Revolutionary Spirits

Revolutionary Spirits

The Enlightened Faith of America's Founding Fathers

Gary Kowalski

BlueBridge

Jacket design by Cynthia Dunne

Cover art top by The Bridgeman Art Library
(Albert Bierstadt [1830–1902], California Sunset*)*

Cover art bottom by The Bridgeman Art Library
(John Trumbull [1756–1843], Signing the Declaration of Independence*)*

Text design by Cynthia Dunne

Library of Congress Cataloging-in-Publication Data

Kowalski, Gary A.
Revolutionary spirits : the enlightened faith of America's founding fathers / Gary Kowalski.
p. cm.
Includes bibliographical references and index.
ISBN-13: 978-1-933346-09-0
ISBN-10: 1-933346-09-4
1. United States—Religion—To 1800. 2. Founding Fathers of the United States—Religious life. I. Title.
BR520.K69 2007
277.3'07—dc22   2007018162

Published by
B l u e B r i d g e
An imprint of
United Tribes Media Inc.
240 West 35th Street, Suite 500
New York, NY 10001

www.bluebridgebooks.com

Printed in the United States of America

10 9 8 7 6 5 4 3 2 1

Contents

For Tid

Revolutionary Spirits

—•◦•◦•—

Introduction

Every year hundreds of thousands of tourists flock to Mount Vernon and Monticello as well as other shrines to the nation's founders, like Constitution Hall and the Franklin Museum in Philadelphia; the Adams homestead in Quincy, Massachusetts; and James Madison's residence, Montpelier, in Virginia. For many, the visits have aspects of a spiritual pilgrimage. Seekers come to gain a sense of the lived and living presence of men who occupy an exalted place in the temple of American civil religion.

The flesh-and-blood figures who inhabited these historical landmarks have long since departed. But, in a sense, they continue to move and breathe in the institutions they established. And few individuals have been more thoroughly studied and documented than all those who made the American Revolution. Yet their underlying humanity, including their private hopes and fears and most profound thoughts about the meaning of it all, remain little appreciated. Who were they in their solitude—when they searched their depths in the presence of their Maker?

The denominational affiliation of the founders ran the gamut. Among the fifty-six who signed the Declaration of Independence, there were Baptists, Congregationalists, Presbyterians, Episcopalians, Quakers, Unitarians, Roman Catholics, and Universalists represented. Haym Salomon, a Polish Jew who immigrated to America in 1772, became an important financier of the Revolution, while other Jews like Major Benjamin Nones were cited for gallantry in arms. In the Continental Army, according to John Adams, "There were among them, Roman Catholicks, English Episcopalians, Scotch and American Presbyterians, Methodists, Moravians, Anabaptists, German Lutherans, German Calvinists, Universalists, Arians, Priestleyans, Socinians, Independents, Congregationalists, Horse Protestants and House Protestants, Deists and Atheists." He might have mentioned there were also both blacks and whites, for the half million Americans of African descent were represented at almost every major battle, usually under the Stars and Stripes although occasionally fighting for the Union Jack. Tories and Patriots were present among almost every religious group, while nonviolent sects like the Friends and Mennonites held themselves aloof from the conflict as a matter of conscience. America was a religious mélange even in the eighteenth century.

Who were these cocky continentals? They were a mixed crew. Some had come to the New World for spiritual reasons, while for others the motives were mainly economic. Among religious refugees, none are more famous than the Pilgrims who landed at Plymouth in 1620, having separated from the Church of England to worship and organize congregations according to their own strict interpretation of the Bible. But even aboard the *Mayflower*, only 40 of the 102 passengers were members of the Pilgrim band. Fourteen were servants, but the rest were nonseparatists recruited from the merchant company that financed the voyage. Within a few years there was a falling out. William Bradford, the God-fearing governor who ruled the colony like an old-fashioned patriarch, relates in his *History of Plymouth Plantation* how the less stringently religious among them—derisively called "strangers" as opposed to "saints"—resented his authority and determined that "they would use their own liberty; for none had power to command them." Under leadership of a Mister Morton, the mutineers established their own plantation with a promise to "live together as equals," where according to Bradford they maintained "a school of Atheism." Soon it became hard for the Pilgrims to keep their hired help; many servants ran away to join the commune at Merrymount where dancing and other amusements were permitted. Something had to be done. Pilgrim John Endicott cut down their maypole, and Captain Miles Standish managed to subdue the rebel outpost. Much as they desired religious liberty for themselves, the Pilgrims were not eager to extend it to others.

The landing at Plymouth encapsulated a story retold

frequently in the colonial period. America was settled by religious dissenters, the overwhelming majority, almost 90 percent, of English extraction. Congregationalists (like the Pilgrims and the Puritans who soon outnumbered and absorbed them) and Presbyterians, who shared much the same theology, were the largest sects, anchored mostly in New England. Baptists and Quakers, more widely dispersed in the middle colonies and the South, also claimed sizeable numbers of adherents. Anglicans flourished in Virginia, while the populations of North Carolina, South Carolina, and Georgia were eclectic, despite episcopal establishments that existed on paper. All of these were Protestant. But in contrast to the mother country, where Anglicans predominated, most Americans had broken away from the Church of England, which they considered to be either wholly or partly corrupt. They were accustomed to defying the king, the titular head of that church. This prepared them for rebellion when the time came. But while they desired freedom for themselves, they could also be narrow and intolerant.

Alongside the Pilgrims and their dissenting kin, however, there were other colonists who were not particularly pious at all. North America was rich in raw materials and, in the eyes of the royal exchequer, needed settlers. So not only religious troublemakers, but other undesirables were encouraged to leave England. These included the destitute and felons—at a time when failing to doff the cap to lord or lady might constitute a criminal offense. Entrepreneurs, adventurers, and vagabonds filled out the ranks of immigrants. Many were what John Adams called "Horse Protestants" or "Protestants who believe nothing," which is to say that they had about as much appreciation for reformed doctrine as Oliver Cromwell's horse, but were certainly not Jews or Catholics. Worship in either Latin or Hebrew was rare in the eighteenth century. Synagogues existed in just five cities prior to the Revolution. Roman Catholics were a minority even in Maryland, where Lord Baltimore had established a haven for his coreligionists. But while Protestantism provided a nominal background for most colonists, the vast majority of Americans—like the larger number of the ship's crew and passengers aboard the *Mayflower*—were unchurched and not eager to submit to any ecclesiastical body that might restrict their personal liberty.

This was the condition that the Anglo-Irish statesman Edmund Burke (1729–97) described in his essay "On Conciliation with the American Colonies," written in 1775 on the outbreak of war. Warning Parliament against pushing too far, he observed that the colonists were "Protestants, and of that kind which is the most adverse to all implicit subjection of mind and opinion." And this was the challenge the founders faced. Their countrymen and -women were of many faiths and no faith. Most didn't even regard themselves as Americans, but as Pennsylvanians or residents of whatever province they inhabited. As to nationality, most considered themselves British, but there were many exceptions to the rule, like Swedish Lutherans, Dutch Reformed, and German-speaking Moravians whose primary allegiance was to their own church and culture. They were protective of their distinctive traditions and fiercely independent, but could also be exclusive in their beliefs. The founders' task was to meld this variety into a union of shared aspirations and commonly held values.

How far they succeeded is a measure of their greatness, and how they did it is the subject of this book. The figures singled out here are representative: Benjamin Franklin (1706–90), George Washington (1732–99), Thomas Paine (1737–1809),

John Adams (1735–1826), Thomas Jefferson (1743–1826), and James Madison (1751–1836). No account of the American Revolution would be complete without a record of their contributions. And to a surprising degree, the personal lives, political intrigues, and spiritual philosophies of these men intertwined. They had many of the same friends, corresponded with each other, read the same authors, and visited in each other's homes. They exchanged condolences in times of grief. As intimates, the sense of betrayal they experienced when quarrels arose was even sharper. Their differences were personal, not merely ideological. But even when they feuded, as often happened, they had more in common than they themselves sometimes realized.

In part, their faith was rooted in America's Protestant, colonial past. Political dissent and religious dissent were connected in their minds. They believed each individual was directly accountable to God alone, not to any emperor or priest. Like the Pilgrims, they were convinced that providence had destined the New World for a special role in history and that their generation stood on the threshold of an auspicious new beginning. But the America they envisioned was not the Puritans' "city on a hill." Unlike the Massachusetts pioneers, they dreamed not of a purified church, where only saints resided, but of a land where strangers were welcome and differences could thrive.

Dissidents by temper, they were also children of the Enlightenment, which made them as unconventional in their religious opinions as they were innovative in their politics. Many were labeled atheists or infidels by their contemporaries—an accusation that was unfair, but contained a tiny grain of truth. For in a certain sense, they were unbelievers. They questioned the accepted verities. They had little use for religion that they considered closed-minded or doctrinaire. Few of them believed in the literal accuracy of the Bible or in the traditional creeds of Christendom. Most regarded dogmas like the Trinity, the Incarnation, and the Atonement as nonsensical or, at best, irrelevant to achieving a virtuous life.

But none of them were scoffers or religious skeptics. They spoke warmly of a Creator and a moral law that governed the universe. America's founders were convinced that both nature and human nature bore the signs of a divine destiny and origin. They were of an irenic disposition—circumspect rather than disputatious in voicing views where people of good conscience might sincerely differ. They preferred to discuss theology in quiet tones, through appeals to reason and common sense, rather than in the pulpit-pounding cadences of the revivalist. Mistrustful of emotions that could turn masses of people into heated mobs, they encouraged cool heads and critical thinking when it came to questions of faith.

Most agreed that spiritual health was better measured by character and conduct than by formal catechisms. How an individual lived was ultimately more important than which church he or she happened to attend, or whether they went to church at all. Deeds mattered more than creeds. And because they understood faith to be inseparable from how a person behaved in the home, town square, and marketplace, no spiritual portrait of these men would be complete without a biographical sketch that outlined their peculiar personalities and shared ambitions. Their faith was embodied in their workaday occupations and lifelong concerns, as scientists, farmers, lawyers, and politicians.

Naturally, some who fought for independence were more orthodox in their opinions. John Jay and Samuel Adams could be cited as patriots who were rather staid in their religious views. Alexander Hamilton also grew increasingly conservative as he aged. But then Hamilton, who called the popular majority "a great beast" and believed America needed a king, was often out of step, politically as well as religiously—more revisionist than revolutionary in spirit. The figures in these pages, in contrast, drew inspiration wherever they could find it—from the Bible certainly (and especially the teachings of Jesus), but also from classical Greek and Roman thinkers, from Freemasonry, and even from the teachings of Confucius. They were broad-minded and wide-ranging in their spiritual tastes.

While the framers of the United States were nonbelievers in some respects, in others they were true believers indeed, for they believed in religious liberty and were almost fanatically opposed to fanaticism. The Thirty Years' War (1618–1648) between the Protestant Union and Catholic League had embroiled all of Europe in a bloodbath that butchered millions. England suffered its own Civil War in the seventeenth century, and while the Glorious Revolution (1688) brought a modicum of breathing room for nonconformists, relations between the Church of England and religious minorities remained brittle. The holy wars of the previous century instilled a determination to quell extremism, or what the founders would have called "enthusiasm." They were apostles of live-and-let-live.

Theirs was also a gospel of self-government. Populists like Paine and Franklin had humble beginnings and shared a common touch. Those from more privileged backgrounds would never have countenanced universal suffrage or catering to public opinion. But even slaveholding southerners like Madison, Washington, and Jefferson were democrats despite themselves, injecting the dream of equality into the national discourse and a foretaste of its reality into America's social landscape. Caste systems, whether based on skin color, sex, or religion, could never again be taken for granted. While they failed to end the subjugation of blacks by whites—with tragic consequences for both races—the founders nonetheless asserted the existence of human rights that were self-validating and universal. They made claims for "life, liberty and the pursuit of happiness" that could not be indefinitely postponed.

Finally, they believed in reason and in the power of unfettered inquiry to cast off ignorance and prejudice, coming closer to the edge of truth. Minds were expanding during their lifetimes as discoveries of deep space and deep time stretched notions of divinity in new, unimaginable directions. In labs and observatories, from Newton to Boyle, the universe was yielding up long-held secrets, and the genius of the age was captured in the motto of Britain's Royal Society, *Nullius in Verba*, which historian Daniel Boorstin translates as "Take nobody's word for it; see for yourself!" In that spirit, the founders favored fact-based arguments and testable hypotheses, trusting in the five senses more than the four evangelists or five books of Moses. Whether investigating the laws of nature or nations, they looked not to timeworn texts but to experiment and their own wealth of worldly experience for answers, in the process producing an experiment unlike any other—the United States of America.

Disciples of tolerance, freedom, and scientific thinking, they affirmed that faith could be a progressive force in human affairs, uniting people of varying beliefs in allegiance to a shared quest for justice and the common good. America's religious diversity owes much to the kind of deity that the founders appealed to in their prayers and the spiritual values they sought to infuse into the young country's public institutions.

The story is told that Thomas Paine once encountered a Swedenborgian who told him that, after being lost for more than four thousand years, a "key" to unlock the hidden meaning of the scriptures had finally been found. Paine listened politely, then rejoined that a key lost so long must be rather rusty. *Revolutionary Spirits* aims to unlock at least a few insights into the minds and hearts of America's originators. Their enlightened faith is key to understanding the spiritual identity of the country. And their core values, though separated from the present by a span of two centuries, have not corroded with time but remain bright and serviceable to use.

As the United States has entered the twenty-first century torn between runaway secularism and resurgent fundamentalism, the founders' approach to faith is worth examining. For this republic was not born through immaculate conception. Its laws and constitutional principles are human contrivances rather than divinely revealed edicts. The country's legal and political foundations are incomprehensible apart from the spiritual and moral convictions of the individuals who laid its cornerstones.

The beliefs of the founders are pivotal to America's distinctiveness. Knowing more about these figures is key to resisting those who would undo their legacy. And understanding the credo of these revolutionary spirits will help preserve the United States' unique and most valuable attainment—nurturing a people whose faith is at once powerful, varied, and free.

2.

Nature's Nation and Nature's God

Liberals and Deists

George Washington never chopped down a cherry tree, and most of us realize that he never threw a silver dollar across the Potomac. But how many know that he deliberately avoided using the word "God" in his public statements or that he was once nearly arrested for not attending church?

Most people know that Benjamin Franklin invented bifocal spectacles and experimented with electricity. He also invented his own private liturgy, rewrote the Lord's Prayer, and espoused an idiosyncratic creed some might find more shocking than any jolt of lightning.

The founders of the United States—men like Thomas Jefferson and John Adams—are instantly recognizable to every American schoolchild from the portraits that hang in classrooms. But much of what we learn about these seminal figures is based on misinformation, particularly when it comes to their most heartfelt beliefs about God, the Bible, and other matters of faith.

What's best about spiritual life in America is owed to them. For this is a pluralistic culture where strong convictions coexist peaceably as perhaps nowhere else on earth. In many parts of the world where religious feeling runs high, sectarian strife is rampant. Faith becomes a divisive force. But the United States is not only one of the most intensely religious nations in the world—it is also the most spiritually diverse. Somehow the country has managed to combine the adage "In God We Trust" with its original motto, *e pluribus unum*—"out of many, one."

How have citizens with such divergent theologies managed for over two hundred years to live amicably side by side? The answer lies in the faith of the founders, who were in their own way deeply spiritual men, but who were also almost all religious liberals in the classic meaning of that term. They were disciples of the English thinker John Locke (1632–1704)—descendants of a political philosophy that believed in restricting the powers of the state within carefully prescribed limits. The legitimate functions of government were closely defined— "to establish justice, provide for the common defense, insure domestic tranquility and promote the general welfare," according to the Constitution's preamble. Protecting "life, health, liberty or possessions" were essential elements of the social compact, according to Locke. But government had no business endorsing a particular religious viewpoint or policing the thoughts of its citizens. Questions of conscience and personal faith were considered private affairs, beyond the reach of interference by the state.

Locke was a theologian as well as a political theorist. He said that our idea of God originated like all valid ideas, by carefully assembling and sifting the evidence of the senses. The Creator's power could be reasonably deduced from the vast scale of the cosmos. This Being's intelligence was also undeniable, having produced conscious beings like ourselves; the cause must be at least as great as the effect. But Locke questioned whether nonrational modes of knowing should be admissible in theology, any more than in history or physics. Revelation should be subordinate to our own critical faculties: "Reason must be our last judge and guide in everything." Persuasion or argument might change someone's religious beliefs, but force could never compel one to assent to a creed that appeared irrational, doubtful, or absurd.

In a constitution based on Lockean principles, therefore, there would be free exercise of religion. Each person had a right to make up his or her own mind about the claims of competing doctrines. At the same time, the state would make no laws that might erect an ecclesiastical establishment or require citizens to support a belief system their own hearts rejected. These would become the fundamental rights embodied in the First Amendment.

It was a formula that proved incredibly successful and that underlies America's unique blend of robust faith and flourishing variety of religious expression. Visiting the country in the

1830s, Alexis de Tocqueville commented that "the religious atmosphere of the country was the first thing that struck me on arrival in the United States," along with "an innumerable multitude of sects." In his native France, there was a state-sponsored church, but people were not nearly so pious. What was the secret behind the amazing spiritual vitality of the United States?

> To find this out, I questioned the faithful of all communions; I particularly sought the society of clergymen, who are the depositories of the various creeds and have a personal interest in their survival. As a practicing Catholic I was particularly close to the Catholic priests, with some of whom I soon established a certain intimacy. I expressed my astonishment and revealed my doubts to each of them; I found that they all agreed with each other except about details; all thought that the main reason for the quiet sway of religion over their country was the complete separation of church and state.

The result could have been predicted. The framers believed that an official hands-off policy toward religion would unleash people's latent spiritual energies, just as a laissez-faire policy toward the economy would unlock the engine of private enterprise.

History has proven them right. In the marketplace of ideas as in the commercial marketplace, people usually operate best in an environment where they can make their own choices. "Men may choose different things," Locke taught, "and yet all choose right." Personalities and preferences vary, but whether the "product" they are acquiring is spiritual or otherwise, people need to think for themselves and judge their best self-interest. Benjamin Franklin made the connection explicit. If businesses thrive in a climate of competition, he wondered, why wouldn't churches do the same?

But the founders were never purists about laissez-faire. Franklin advocated heavy levies on the rich to promote the common good, for example. Thomas Paine went further; he lobbied for a progressive income tax and inheritance tax, believed in a safety net for workers laid off due to downturns in the business cycle, and felt that families with young children ought to receive a government stipend to help them find their start in life. Regulation of the markets was certainly permissible for some purposes.

And the boundary marking the proper division between church and state was never a bright line, either. At the request of Congress, George Washington declared the 26th of November, 1789, a day of Thanksgiving, inviting the people of the United States to offer "prayers and supplications to the great Lord and Ruler of Nations." John Adams recommended a national day of fasting during his presidency. And when he was appointed to a commission to help design the Great Seal of the United States, Thomas Jefferson initially suggested the seal bear an image of Moses leading the Israelites out of Egypt with an inscription reading "Resistance to Tyrants Is Obedience to God." The founders were certainly religious men, who believed that human liberty, including the rights of conscience, had been divinely ordained. But however blurred the line might become, establishing religious freedom was always their aim—never establishing a particular religion.

Yet liberalism has always had its detractors—then as now—who feel it is the government's job to meddle in spiritual matters. From the very beginning, there were many opposed to the separation of church and state. Just as eighteenth-century mercantilists thought government should favor particular industries over others (protecting manufacturing in England while discouraging it in the colonies, for example), some religious conservatives felt that certain churches, or Christianity in general, should have a preferred status under the law. They were unhappy with the Constitution's strictly neutral stance toward religion.

Some objected to Article Six of the Constitution, which guarantees that "no religious test shall ever be required as a qualification to any office or public trust under the United States." This represented a major change from the practice in Great Britain, where members of dissenting sects like Quakers, Presbyterians, Methodists, and Unitarians were unable to hold public office. When George III took the throne in 1760, only Anglicans were entitled to the full privileges of English citizenship, and some Americans wanted similar restrictions in their newly independent nation. During its state convention to ratify the federal Constitution, a Virginia initiative tried to change the wording and intent of this clause to "no *other* religious test shall ever be required *than* a belief in the one only true God, who is the rewarder of the good, and the punisher of evil." This change was rejected. James Madison wisely defended Article Six as welcoming people of every belief and background into the field of public service: "The door of the Federal Government is open to men of every description, whether native or adoptive, whether young or old, and without regard to poverty or wealth, or to any particular profession of religious faith." And while Madison and the other founders ultimately carried the day, their opponents continued to press for the insertion of more doctrinaire, confessional language into the Constitution.

The designers of the Constitution were emphatic that government derived its authority from the consent of the governed—from "we the people"—and not from any supernatural agency. These were lawyers at work, not clergy, after all. John Adams called the United States "the first example of government erected on the simple principles of nature." The framers never "had interviews with the gods or were in any degree under the inspiration of heaven," he cautioned. But others were of a more theocratic bent. The Reverend John Mason of New York lamented in 1793 that "from the Constitution of the United States, it is impossible to ascertain what God we worship, or whether we own a God at all." A leading cleric from Kentucky fretted in 1815 that although America was "confessedly a Christian nation," the fact was sadly unacknowledged in the nation's charter.

The omission was intentional. Some of America's founders were Christians and others were not. All believed in God, after their own fashion. But their intent was never to establish a godly commonwealth or Christian nation. Rather, America was conceived as nature's nation—a voluntary contract among disparate people living in what John Locke would have called "a state of nature" to form a civil society, governed by the ballot rather than the Bible. Fostering freedom, not saving souls, was the framers' aim. For whatever the precise nature of their personal beliefs, they were as liberal in their religious views as in their political and economic aspirations.

This is news to many contemporary Americans, for "liberal" is a term that has been tarnished, yet it is a label the nation's forefathers wore with pride. When a committee of Roman

Catholics wrote to George Washington at the time of his first inauguration, wondering how religious minorities would be treated under the new administration, he assured them that "as mankind becomes more liberal," distinctions between Catholic, Protestant, and Jew would yield to the precept that all are "equally entitled to the protection of civil government." To a Jewish congregation voicing similar concerns, his answer was the same, applauding the "enlarged and liberal policy" that granted every American the private rights of conscience, along with the public immunities of citizenship.

A liberal is one who cherishes liberty, and freedom was never far from the founders' thoughts. In the political realm, liberalism has been the historic protector and promoter of human rights, carving out a zone of personal autonomy exempt from government intrusion or oversight. Culturally, liberals prize pluralism. A multiplicity of creeds and customs is the hallmark of a healthy society. In the spiritual domain, liberalism has been characterized by an attitude more inquisitive than inquisitorial, believing that religious truth best emerges from the free play of imagination and ideas. In all its forms, liberalism chafes against unwarranted restrictions on the human spirit. With Jefferson, who pledged "eternal hostility to every tyranny over the mind of man," liberals are antiauthoritarian. They are less obedient to the claims of tradition, more receptive to the prospect of improving on the past. To paraphrase historian Peter Gay, liberals fear change less than they fear stagnation.

"Progressive" is a label that fits almost as well as "liberal," for America's founders believed in the doctrine of progress. Everywhere they looked, life was becoming safer, more humane. Child mortality declined in the eighteenth century, and longevity soared as epidemic diseases like typhoid were practically eradicated. Devices like the sextant and more accurate clocks were enabling wandering travelers for the first time to determine their actual locations, while the hot air balloon and submarine were taking them to destinations they'd never dreamed. Human ingenuity appeared to be opening the door to a brighter future, especially in the realm of science and invention—this in an age when educated laypeople could not only comprehend the latest theories, but when amateurs might still make important advances of their own.

To encourage the pursuit of "Useful Knowledge" among such gentlemen scholars, Benjamin Franklin in 1769 founded the American Philosophical Society, modeled on Britain's Royal Society, for the promotion of basic research. Standing committees encompassed the range: anatomy and medicine; mathematics and astronomy; chemistry, geography, and natural history; botany and horticulture; as well as applied fields like architecture and economics.

In addition to Franklin, whose work in physics won him worldwide fame, Washington and Adams, Jefferson, Madison, and Paine were all members of the Philosophical Society, subscribing and occasionally contributing to the *Transactions* where learned papers were exchanged. Washington conducted controlled experiments at his Mount Vernon estate, constructing a box with multiple compartments where he could plant grains in various types of soil, each at the same depth, and observe the effect of differing fertilizers on their growth. The instrument maker David Rittenhouse, who succeeded Franklin as president of the Philosophical Society, created an "orrery" or clockwork miniature of the solar system for Princeton University that would inspire a young James Madison, who later naturally reached for Newtonian metaphors to describe how checks and balances could stabilize government, just as the counterpoise of gravity and inertia brought equilibrium to planetary motion. Thomas Jefferson, when he traveled to Philadelphia to take up his duties as the nation's vice president in 1797, carried with him a collection of fossils to illustrate a scheduled lecture on paleontology before his Philosophical Society colleagues. John Adams, who established the American Academy of Arts and Sciences, was just as fascinated with astronomy. Seldom have any group of statesmen been so enamored with "philosophical Experiments that let Light into the Nature of Things."

It gave them an international outlook. The American Philosophical Society included participants from all over the colonies and abroad. Science (more often called "natural philosophy" or simply "philosophy") was becoming the world's lingua franca. The founders were inspired by the spirit of cooperation that prevailed in 1761 and again in 1769, for example, during the effort to observe the transit of Venus, when astronomers from France, Britain, Denmark, Germany, Italy, Spain, Portugal, the Netherlands, and the American colonies pooled measurements from sixty-two sites around the globe to produce the first truly accurate measurements of the solar system. Though France and Britain were at war, hostilities ceased long enough to allow Captain Cook to continue his voyage to Tahiti to take readings from the South Pacific. During the war for independence, Benjamin Franklin wrote Cook a passport providing safe passage through waters controlled by American warships in order to further his explorations, directing commanders to refrain from plunder but rather to "treat the said Captain Cook and his people with all civility and kindness."

As world citizens, their connections spanned the continents. Franklin and Cook had become friends when the American was ambassador in London. Though his poor health prevented travel, James Madison became an honorary citizen of France. Other founders—Adams, Jefferson, and British-born Paine—spent years living abroad and were acquainted with the great scientists of Europe. During the Napoleonic wars, Thomas Jefferson actually suggested transporting the entire Genevan Academy away from the battlefields of Europe to the safer shores of America to pursue their investigations unmolested. Franklin's hope that a philosopher might soon be able to set foot anywhere in the world and say "this is my country" expressed an optimism that a truly planetary culture might be emerging.

If religion had produced more bloodshed than brotherhood in the past, perhaps a faith based on experimentalism and reason might finally unite humankind, imparting truths on which disinterested seekers could all concur. The cosmos presented a folio of order and regularity signed in the Creator's own hand, a testament prior to any written scripture (literally old as the hills). Not every chapter and verse of the Bible could be read there, of course. America's founders sensed the sacred in the laws and harmonies of nature, rather than in the miraculous suspension of those laws. Still, delving into the book of nature was a means of understanding the thoughts of its divine Author, and when they referred to a deity it was most often under the rubric of Chief Architect or Grand Designer—the God revealed in the workings of earth and sky rather than the traditional God of Abraham and Isaac. This proclivity to approach God through the phenomena of nature rather than via revelation is often called Deism—a term that to some degree fits most of these founders. They worshiped in the cathedral of Creation.

Nature was not only the object of scientific study, but also the subject of serene meditation. Deists could wax lyrical, like Thomas Paine:

> One of the finest scenes and subjects of religious contemplation is to walk into the woods and fields, and survey the works of the God of Creation. The wide expanse of heaven, the earth covered with verdure, the lofty forest, the waving corn, the magnificent roll of mighty rivers, and the murmuring melody of the cheerful brooks, are scenes that inspire the mind with gratitude and delight.

More often, they were matter-of-fact, like James Madison in his nature journals, which included entries like "Wild geese flying N.ward" and "Blue hyacinths bloom." For devotees of natural religion, the holy was not remote, but a warm and living presence—the Creator's beneficence as close as migrating birds (Madison wondered how far north cardinals range) or flowers about the dooryard.

God was artist as well as engineer. With tastes running strongly toward wilderness scenes, George Washington chose for his banquet hall at Mount Vernon two landscapes by George Beck, known for his outdoor sketches, depicting "Falls of the Potomac" and "The Potomac Near Harper's Ferry." For European readers, Jefferson described the passage of the mighty river through the Alleghenies as alternately "placid and delightful" and "wild and tremendous," a scene well worth a trip across the Atlantic. "It is impossible for the emotions arising from the sublime, to be felt beyond what they are here," he wrote of another geological wonder, praising the natural bridge near his home as "so beautiful an arch, so elevated, so light," that it induced indescribable raptures in the spectator. In a less elevated vein, he noticed that the creek passing under the bridge was sufficient to turn a gristmill even in dry weather. Theirs was a benign deity who made the world not only breathtaking, but useful as well.

Like modern scientists, these were men of a practical temper. They were less interested in metaphysical speculation than in solving down-to-earth problems, whether building a more efficient stove or an improved plow or creating a better judiciary. They liked questions that could be answered. And in religious terms, this meant that many of the founders were content to leave insoluble questions alone. "The finiteness of the human understanding betrays itself on all subjects," as James Madison remarked, "but more especially when it contemplates such as involve infinity." They were comfortable with ambiguity and able to respond to many theological riddles—from the nature of the Godhead to the divinity of Christ—with a genial agnosticism.

While most Deists entertained some hopes for an afterlife, the precise form that eternity might take remained an enigma for many. Creating a better life in this world seemed more important than preparing for the next one. "It has been long, very long, a settled opinion in my Mind that there is now, never will be, and never was but one being who can Understand the Universe," John Adams wrote to Thomas Jefferson. Jefferson returned the sentiment. Asked about his thoughts on life after death and the immortality of the soul, the man from Monticello responded:

> When I was young I was fond of the speculations which seemed to promise some insight into that hidden country, but observing at length that they left me in the same

ignorance in which they had found me, I have for very many years ceased to read or to think concerning them, and have reposed my head on that pillow of ignorance which a benevolent Creator has made so soft for us, knowing how much we should be forced to use it.

It was vain for creatures like ourselves to pretend to know all the answers.

At the same time, the founders believed emphatically that some questions *could* be answered; they possessed the greatest faith in education as a tool that could mold and uplift society. These were men who founded universities (including the University of Pennsylvania and the University of Virginia), endowed libraries (including the Library of Congress), published newspapers, and produced some of the world's bestselling literature, from *The Rights of Man* to *The Federalist Papers*. A school teacher before he became a lawyer, John Adams took special care for the instruction of his own offspring, assuring Abigail that "the virtues and powers to which men may be trained by early education and constant discipline are truly sublime and astonishing."

The fact that many of the founders were home-schooled or self-educated only confirmed their vision of the potential to create an enlightened populace. George Washington never went to college. Paine and Franklin had only the most rudimentary formal education. At the beginning of the eighteenth century, many children were expected to go to work as early as age six. But by 1779, Thomas Jefferson had formulated one of the earliest plans for free, universal public schools, from primary grades through college, arguing that "if a nation expects to be ignorant and free, in a state of civilization, it expects what never was and never will be." After the Revolution, literacy and an informed citizenry came to be seen as pillars of self-government. That was why Washington, in his Farewell Address, encouraged posterity to promote "institutions for the general diffusion of knowledge." And in his last will and testament, Washington made no bequests to any churches, but he did provide for a free school for orphans, as well as establish an endowment for a national university to educate students in the "principles of Politics and good Government."

The founders tended to be interested in religion for the same reason they supported education, as a means toward fostering a more peaceful, prosperous, and ethically minded republic. They believed virtue would gradually replace vice as surely as knowledge displaced ignorance and philosophy outpaced superstition. With good sense ruling the mind, good conduct would indubitably follow. Civilization would progress.

So the forecast for the future seemed upbeat. "When I contemplate the immense advances in science and discoveries in the arts which have been made in the period of my life, I look forward with confidence to equal advances by the present generation," Thomas Jefferson predicted in 1818, "and have no doubt they will consequently be as much wiser than we have been as we than our fathers were, and they than the burners of witches."

But those burning times were not so far in the past.

3.

Beyond Black Arts
and Witchcraft

The Progress of Enlightenment

Historians debate the precise date when the Middle Ages ended. But at some point, a Christian civilization with an otherworldly orientation became increasingly focused on the here and now. Educated people stopped looking to the ancients—Aristotle and the Church Fathers—as the ultimate sources of knowledge and grew confident of their own ability to find things out. Magic was replaced by technology. The pre-Copernican universe was discarded, and as notions of the heavens changed, the belief that some men ruled others by heavenly decree became the relic of an antiquated past. Assumptions that had gone unchallenged since time immemorial suddenly appeared old-fashioned and oddly out-of-date.

In North America, this intellectual awakening dawned just over three hundred years ago. January 17, 1706, is a date as close as any to being a defining moment. That's when Benjamin Franklin was born. And between his birth, at the opening of the eighteenth century, and the date when John Adams and Thomas Jefferson both died, on July 4, 1826, America's cultural and religious landscape was transfigured. A new world sprang into being. The half million settlers strung in a thin line along the eastern seaboard at the beginning of this period exploded into a population of twelve million in twenty-one states as first Vermont, then Kentucky, Tennessee, Ohio, Louisiana, Mississippi, Alabama, and Maine joined the Union. The war for independence and the establishment of the new Constitution were the defining military and political events of the epoch. But in science, education, medicine, law, and the life of the spirit, equally important revolutions were taking place.

The medieval world was dying, while a more contemporary outlook was struggling to emerge. The Enlightenment was spreading its glow, not only among *philosophes*, but on the level of everyday explanations of how the world worked. Fear of the supernatural was waning. Belief in astrology was in decline as celestial motions and occurrences were demystified. Mental illness, which had been associated with demon possession, was coming to be seen in more helpful and compassionate terms as a malady with physiological origins. Geographical maps were becoming more accurate, and people's mental maps grew less fearful. The credulity of an earlier age was being replaced by an outlook that valued critical thinking.

Needless to say, the founders of the republic helped to shape all these trends and were shaped by them in turn.

Beliefs about sorcery were indicative of broader currents of change. When four children in his parish began experiencing convulsions in Boston, their Puritan minister Cotton Mather (1663–1728) concluded that the youngsters were "sadly molested with Evil Spirits." The woman who enchanted them was duly tried. Naturally, she was hanged, for there was practically no defense against "spectral evidence" and the presumption was guilty until proven innocent. *Memorable Providences, Relating to Witchcraft and Possessions* (1689), Mather's lurid account of the affair, helped excite the hysteria that took place three years later in the neighboring town of Salem, where twenty people and two dogs were executed, with hundreds more accused, imprisoned, and held awaiting trial. Though the whole frightening episode was called a "delusion" by Thomas Brattle, one of the more liberal thinkers among the Puritan divines, the killing didn't end until the judges themselves were in danger of going to the gallows.

Nineteen of the victims were hanged, but one, Giles Corey, was pressed to death for refusing to plead either "guilty" or "not guilty," making it impossible to begin the trial. He was crushed beneath increasingly heavy weights, dying over the course of two days. Torture was in common use to extract confessions. Trial by ordeal was also a frequent operating procedure. The accused might be tossed into a pond or river with her hands tied. If the victim sank, she was pronounced innocent. If she floated, the water had "rejected" her and her guilt was assured. Either way, the end result was the same. But trial by ordeal was going out of fashion. When a mob of villagers in Hertfordshire, England, "floated" Ruth Osborne on the charge of consorting with the devil in 1751, the ringleaders of the gang that drowned the poor woman were themselves tried and convicted of murder.

America's founders were among those who helped stamp out the witch craze once and for all. Readers of the *Pennsylvania Gazette* on October 22, 1731, for example, were astonished to learn of an incident supposedly witnessed by three hundred people in nearby Burlington, New Jersey, where a man and woman had been indicted on allegations of sorcery. Charges against the two included "making their neighbour's sheep dance in an uncommon manner, and with causing hogs to speak, and sing Psalms, &c. To the great terror and amazement of the King's good and peaceable subjects in this province." Arrangements were made to put them to the test. In the first ordeal, the two would be weighed in a scale against a Bible. If Holy Writ "weighed in" against them, it would prove that the two were indeed practitioners of the black arts. The second ordeal involved "floating." Anxious to vindicate their innocence, the pair readily consented to these conditions, but insisted that two of their accusers accompany them in trial.

One at a time, the four were placed upon a scale. All were heavier than the books of Moses, the Prophets, and Apostles put together. "Flesh and Bones came down plump, and outweighed that great good Book by abundance." No deviltry was evident. "This being over, the Accusers and the rest of the Mob, not satisfied with this Experiment, would have the Trial by Water; accordingly a most solemn Procession was made to the Mill-pond; where both Accused and Accusers were stripp'd (saving only to the Women their Shifts) were bound Hand and Foot, and severally placed in the Water."

One of the accusers, a rather thin man, began to sink, while the rest bobbed to the surface. Alarmed to find herself so buoyant, the other accuser asked that she be dunked, believing that "the Accused had bewitched her to make her so light, and that she would be duck'd again a Hundred Times, but she would duck the Devil out of her." A sailor in the crowd jumped onto the back of the alleged Wizard, meaning to submerge him and drive him to the bottom. But the unfortunate fellow resurfaced like a cork and "being surpriz'd at his own Swimming, was not so confident of his Innocence as before, but said, 'If I am a Witch, it is more than I know.'" The more thoughtful spectators were skeptical of these shenanigans, reasoning that "unless they were mere Skin and Bones" any person bound and thrown into a body of water would swim "till their Breath was gone, and their Lungs fill'd with Water." However, a larger number present believed the women's shifts and garters helped them float and determined they should be tried again, naked, as soon as the weather grew warmer.

But don't believe everything you read in the papers—particularly not the *Pennsylvania Gazette*. The entire episode was a fabrication invented by Benjamin Franklin to poke fun at the outlandish notions of yokels who believed in necromancy. Satire, he found, was often a more effective weapon against the follies of the ignorant than launching a head-on assault. Yet well into the eighteenth century, witchcraft remained no laughing matter.

As a thirty-four-year-old attorney, John Adams defended John Ames of West Boxford, Massachusetts, who had been accused of murdering his wife, Ruth. The two had been married in December of 1768 and moved together to the home of his parents. The bride was already with child; the marriage was off to a bad start. The next spring, a baby was born to the couple, and shortly afterward the young mother died under circumstances that led to neighbors' suspicions and calls for an inquest.

At the hearing, the church—which doubled as the court-house—was "much thronged by a promiscuous multitude of people." After opening with a prayer, the coroners then led the crowd up to the cemetery, where Ruth had been hastily bur-ied five weeks before, to exhume the body. Short on entertain-ment, gawkers pushed forward to see the grisly remains. The autopsy revealed that Ruth Ames "came to her death by Felony (that is to say by poison) given to her by a Person or Persons to us unknown," but her husband and his mother were the prime suspects. Both were locked up, pending trial.

Many years before, Mr. Ames's grandmother Rebecca had been convicted of witchcraft and condemned to death in Salem—where his own case was now to be heard. Because there was no real evidence to convict anyone, the judge in charge decided that the issue might be settled through Ordeal by Touch.

Based upon an old English and Scottish superstition known as "Bier Right," this bit of folklore held that the wounds of a corpse would begin to bleed anew if touched by the mur-derer. Shakespeare alludes to it in his play *Richard III*. When a guilty Gloucester interrupts the funeral of Henry VI, Lady Anne cries:

O gentlemen, see, see! Dead Henry's wounds
Open their congealed mouths and bleed afresh.

The "unnatural deed" was supposed to excite a supernatural response from the dead body. The technique was tried-and-true; it had often been employed in the Massachusetts Bay Colony. In 1646, for instance, a woman named Mary Martin found herself in the age-old predicament of being pregnant and unwed. In her case, unfortunately, the father was already married. When the time came, Mary said her baby was delivered stillborn, but infanticide seemed more likely. Before a jury, the mother was commanded to touch the face of her deceased child. When she did, "the blood came fresh to it," after which she made a full confession and was sentenced to be hanged. In a macabre ending, according to Governor Winthrop, after poor Mary "had hung a space, she spake, and asked what they did mean to do. Then some stepped up, and turned the knot of the rope backward, and then she soon died."

Now, over a hundred years later, Ordeal by Touch was again being invoked to determine guilt or innocence. Ruth Ames's body was laid out upon a table with a sheet over it. The accused were told to place their index fingers upon the dead woman's neck. At this point, the attorney for the defense objected loudly. John Adams was aghast at the proceedings and refused to let his client touch his wife's body, declaring that "This is nothing but black-arts and witchcraft!" Ames was acquitted of the murder charge, and it was the last time that witchcraft wormed its way into a Massachusetts court of law. If the framers were committed to due process—building into the Constitution the right to trial by jury, protection from self-incrimination, prohibition of cruel and unusual punishment, the right to counsel and to cross-examine witnesses—it was for good reason. The mania of Salem was not so far in the past.

The Enlightenment brought an end to witch-hunting and

also undermined America's widespread fascination with astrology. Horoscopes from this period are found mainly in almanacs, which at the beginning of the eighteenth century were almost as common as Bibles. Although not strictly in opposition to the teachings of the church, they offered an alternative to divine providence in explaining the apportionment of good and bad fortune here on earth. Most households owned one. Between 1639, when America's first *Almanack Calculated for New England* rolled off the press, and the close of the next century, well over a thousand different almanacs were published in the New World. As the numbers suggest, almanacs were a highly popular genre, filled with weather reports, medicinal tips, and farming advice suitable for every season of the year, as well as with more fantastic prophecies.

Almost all of them also contained a figure known as the "Zodiac Man," whose anatomy corresponded to the various signs of the horoscope. In America, he also went by other names: the Man of Signs, moon's man, or the "naked man." Colonial diaries indicate that horoscopes were cast for a variety of purposes: as love charms or to reap a bumper crop. One farmer experiencing a poor yield complained that "nothing has grown this week. It's my 3^{d} planet that governs, and I shall not this year amount to a groat."

Some of these volumes made an attempt to give a scientific basis for their prognostications. As the author of one such work explained:

> Astrology has a Philosophical Foundation: the celestial Powers that can and do agitate and move the whole Ocean, have also Force and Ability to change and alter the Fluids and Solids of the humane Body, and that which can alter

and change the fluids and Solids of the Body, must also greatly affect and influence the Mind; and that which can and does affect the Mind, has a great Share and Influence in the Actions of Men.

A Connecticut clergyman actually carried out experiments to prove that pruning shrubbery had best results under the sign of Leo. But most almanacs simply ascribed planetary influence on human affairs to occult forces, with no causal link between the celestial events and their terrestrial counterparts. Samuel Clough's almanac of 1706, for instance, commented that a lunar eclipse "doth fore-show a continuance of Wars, motions of Armies by Land, and Fleets by Sea, great Slaughters of men, Tumultes, Seditions, Captivities, Treacherous Plots and Devices." How or why the earth's shadow moving across the lunar surface portended such dire consequences was left unsaid. The question was never raised, much less given a satisfactory answer.

The omission is understandable, for most almanacs still held to a Ptolemaic cosmology where the earth occupied the center of the universe. Nathaniel Bowen's almanac of 1722, for instance, informed readers that "The Heavens are Transparent Orbs which are suppos'd extended as great Vaults or Arches round about the Earth, and one within another, and are Eleven in Number." It was a sentence that could have been written a thousand years earlier. The idea that the earth revolved around the sun hadn't yet penetrated the brain of the average dairymaid or field hand. In terms of how they understood the universe, many Americans at the beginning of the eighteenth century were still living in the Middle Ages, or before.

But that was about to change. Benjamin Franklin's *Poor Richard's Almanack*, penned under the name of Richard

Saunders, became one of the best-selling books in the American colonies. Published continuously from 1732 to 1757, print runs typically ran to ten thousand copies. As might be expected, Franklin's learning shone through. The edition for 1753 still contains a depiction of the "Zodiac Man" in the frontpiece, as a concession to popular culture perhaps. But the remainder of the book is devoted to an elucidation of the heavens based on the latest astronomical research. Under the month of February, he explained that "Astronomers know certainly the Distance of the Moon from the Earth, viz. 240 thousand Miles, because the Moon yields a very Sensible Parallax; and they know, that the Sun's Distance from the Earth is very probably, and at least, ten thousand Times the Diameter or Thickness of the Earth, which is about eight thousand Miles, and brings the Whole Distance to about eighty Millions of Miles." These calculations would be enormously refined in 1761, he continued, when astronomers across the world would make precise measurements of the planet Venus as it crossed the solar disk. (The distance to the sun would be revised to 93 million miles at that time, closer to its actual value.) Approximate or not, Franklin's computations showed that our universe was much larger than previously imagined and that human beings occupied just a tiny portion of it.

However, many Americans still needed to be convinced that the Earth revolved around the sun, rather than vice versa. *Poor Richard's* introduced such readers to the world of Copernicus and Galileo in easy-to-understand lessons. If the Earth really moves through space, some wondered, why wouldn't stuff just fly off the surface? In the July section of the 1753 almanac, Franklin explained how a heavy object, dropped from the mast of a sailing ship, would be carried along with the moving vessel rather than falling behind into the water because it shared the boat's impetus. Just so with people, animals, and other items on spaceship Earth. The page for August contained a simple tutorial on how the seasons are produced by the tilt of Earth's axis, and in October, Franklin illumined the workings of a solar eclipse, inviting readers to use candles and apples to observe how the moon might occlude the sun's light. Without fully grasping Newton's laws of gravitation or the mathematical breakthroughs that were redefining time and space, a general audience with *Poor Richard's* help could still get the basics of celestial mechanics.

Franklin made sure his audience understood the superiority of the new astronomy by lampooning the system it was replacing:

> Ignorant Men wonder how we Astrologers foretell the Weather so exactly, unless we deal with the old black Devil. Alas! 'tis as easy as pissing abed. For Instance; The Stargazer spies perhaps VIRGO (or the Virgin;) she turns her Head round as it were to see if any body observ'd her; then crouching down gently, with her Hands on her Knees, she looks wistfully for a while right forward. He judges rightly what she's about: And having calculated the Distance and allow'd Time for it's Falling, finds that next Spring we shall have a fine April shower.

Astrologers didn't actually explain rainfall as celestial urination, but the joke was effective nonetheless. With each successive printing of *Poor Richard's Almanack* and others like it, the old ways of thinking were beginning to seem more primitive, holdovers from a benighted past.

Astrology still had its adherents—Dolley Madison for one. Congratulating a friend on a new arrival, she gushed, "May the horoscope of your young daughter be the most happy; may the bright aspect of her destiny be chronicled in unerring lines." Dolley also consulted fortune-tellers from time to time. But astronomy—not astrology—and meteorology became the subjects enshrined in university curricula, and her better-educated husband James kept a daily "weather diary" to establish temperature predictions based on altitude, latitude, and distance from the sea. Casting horoscopes to forecast rain was passé. Among learned people, a consensus was building that natural phenomena were best explained by naturalistic causes.

That outlook was also gaining currency in the practice of medicine, particularly in the field of psychiatry. Madmen were abused like animals or punished like criminals up until the beginning of the eighteenth century. When Connecticut opened its first state prison in 1727, the inmates included not only "all rogues, vagabonds and idle persons going about in town or country begging," but also "persons under distraction" who were automatically whipped on the bare back upon admission. Sometimes the "distracted" were locked into the cellars or attics of private homes or chained in outbuildings. On Sundays, jailers charged admission for a glimpse of the wretches under their care. Because clergy often doubled as doctors during the early colonial period, insanity tended to be seen as a moral or spiritual affliction, requiring punishment or purgation, rather than as a medical condition inviting treatment. The pillory, where lunatics could be exposed to ridicule in the town square, was put to frequent use.

The American physician Benjamin Rush (1745–1813) was among those who helped bring psychiatry out of the dark ages. Born in Pennsylvania, Rush had studied medicine in London and Edinburgh, returning to his native land to accept the appointment as a professor of chemistry at the newly organized College of Philadelphia, just in time to plunge into the revolutionary cause as a delegate to the Continental Congress. Like his close friends Franklin, Jefferson, and Adams, he was among the original signers of the Declaration of Independence. He served as physician general of the Middle Department of the Continental Army. And like other revolutionary spirits, he, too, was a liberal in religion. Affiliated with the Quakers, Presbyterians, Episcopalians, and Universalists at differing points in his life, Rush described his faith as "a compound of the orthodoxy and heterodoxy of most of our Christian churches." That faith fit together comfortably with his scientific interests. In addition to his lectures on chemistry, he spoke authoritatively on topics like "An Inquiry into the natural history of medicine among the Indians of North America, and a comparative view of their diseases and remedies with those of civilized nations," as well as penning wide-ranging essays on slavery (he was against it) and universal education (which he supported for both sexes). Rush wrote to John Adams that he tried to apply to theology the same "spirit of inquiry" he had learned in the practice of medicine. And that same inquisitive spirit made him ask if there were not more effective and humane methods for dealing with the unfortunates in his care.

When Rush joined the staff of the Pennsylvania Hospital at the age of thirty-eight, he found patients chained to metal rings in the basement floors. Some were handcuffed or bound in straitjackets ("madd-shirts"). Orderlies delivered lashings to maintain discipline in surroundings that Rush described as freezing in winter, stifling in hot weather, dark and noisome at all times.

At Rush's behest, proper bathrooms were installed, with a pump for water. Those able to work were set at liberty to engage in what would today be called occupational therapy: gardening, sewing, carpentry, and weaving. At the doctor's insistence, patients were treated with dignity and properly dressed, rather than clothed in filth and rags. "For many centuries," Rush lamented, the mentally deranged had "been treated like criminals, or shunned like beasts of prey; or, if visited, it has only been for the purpose of inhuman curiosity and amusement." But under his stewardship, the hospital was reborn:

> The clanking of chains, and the noise of the whip, are no longer heard in their cells. They now taste of the blessings of air, and light and motion, in pleasant and shaded walks in summer, and in spacious entries, warmed by stove, in winter, in both of which the sexes are separated and alike protected from the eye of the visitors of the Hospital. In consequence of these advantages, they have recovered the human figure, and with it, their long forgotten relationship to their friends and the public.

Rush was convinced that mental disturbances were like bodily ailments, theorizing that "the cause of madness is seated primarily in the blood-vessels of the brain, and that it depends upon the same kind of morbid and irregular actions that constitute other arterial diseases." While he was wrong about the details, the important point he endeavored to prove in *Medical Inquiries and Observations, upon the Diseases of the Mind*, which became a standard textbook on the subject, was that "the mind and body are moved by the same causes and subject to the same laws." Psychological disturbances ought to be looked on as illnesses rather than as demonic outbursts or character defects.

Up until then, physical and mental disabilities had been considered forms of divine chastisement. Cotton Mather, for example, confided to his diaries a sense of personal sin and guilt because he suffered from a lifelong stutter—a handicap he regarded as punishment from God. Birth deformities were popularly believed to result from intercourse with the devil. By stressing the natural causes of illness, the new model of disease removed the stigma accompanying such ailments. Sufferers deserved compassion rather than condemnation. There was no longer any shame in getting sick—and no penalties should be attached.

Insanity might therefore be a legal defense, Rush ventured—not only if the accused were incapable of telling right from wrong, but if they were driven to their crime by an overpowering impulse. Equally innocent were those laboring under religious delusions—who mistakenly believed themselves to be God or the Messiah—or who uttered blasphemies in an unbalanced state of mind. "There was a time when persons thus deranged were subjected to fines, imprisonment, the extirpation of their tongues, and even to death from fire and the halter," Rush observed. In reality, they were no more guilty of impiety than those experiencing an epileptic fit.

Is it any wonder that individuals like Rush felt themselves to be living in a period of progress? Enlightenment thinkers in America and abroad were working to reform the penal code, hatching schemes for universal education, and harnessing the powers of nature for the benefit of human well-being. Their optimism about the future blinded them sometimes. Slavery, for example, was an evil that made all the founders uneasy. John and Abigail Adams were careful to hire only free labor on their farm; Franklin and Paine actively agitated for abolition. But even those who owned slaves were convinced slavery was a barbarism that would be ameliorated and eventually outgrown. For men like Jefferson and Madison, the certainty that tomorrow would be more civilized than yesterday or today defused their sense of urgency. They were content to leave the heavy lifting of ending human bondage to coming generations, and it was their greatest moral failure. But in other respects, Americans of the eighteenth century were energized by the improvements they saw around them. A worldwide movement was afoot. New nations were being launched. Old institutions were being retooled. And everywhere, the frontiers of knowledge were pushing back the terror of the unknown.

Even the geography of the planet was becoming less fearsome and more accessible. In 1803, Samuel Miller remarked in his *Retrospect of the Eighteenth Century* that "At the beginning of the century [ca. 1700] almost half the surface of the globe was either entirely unknown, or the knowledge of it was so small and indistinct, as to be of little practical value. Since that time such discoveries and improvements have been made, that geography has assumed a new face, and become almost a new science." Despite the circumnavigation of Magellan and other voyages of previous ages, the interior reaches of North and South America were mostly terra incognita to colonists who first arrived at Jamestown and Plymouth. As late as 1707, Cotton Mather warned his countrymen not only of the "rabid and Howling wolves" that inhabited the woodlands of New England, but also of the "Dragons, Droves of Devils, and Fiery Flying Serpents" that waited to pounce on the unwary.

A scant seventy-five years later, Thomas Jefferson could compile a comprehensive listing of the quadrupeds of North America in his *Notes on the State of Virginia*, a model of zoological thoroughness that carefully enumerates indigenous species ranging from the tapir to the caribou. It goes without saying, no "Fiery Flying Serpents" made the list.

It wasn't that Mather was ignorant. He was a highly intelligent person—some would say brilliant—voicing the received opinions of his time. But times were changing. And the men who were bringing America into being were also busy relegating the Reverend Mather's creatures of fantasy to the dustbin of a premodern past. The founders were busy constructing a modern nation that would serve as inspiration for a world aching to throw off a medieval heritage of cruelty and oppression—replacing fanaticism with careful rules of evidence, superstition with solid science, and fear of the unknown with faith in humanity's ability to explore and find out.

Who were these individuals—and what did they really believe?

4.

A Reasonable Creature

The Faith of Benjamin Franklin

Cotton Mather and Benjamin Franklin were contemporaries. They were also neighbors in Boston, and while the Puritan preacher was more than old enough to be Ben's father, they walked the same crooked streets, laid out by the cows that grazed the Common. As a boy of eleven, Benjamin read Mather's *Essays to Do Good*, and the book made a favorable impression. A few years later, Franklin actually went to visit the great clergyman. As he was leaving the house, Mather shouted at him, "Stoop! Stoop!" but the warning came too late and Franklin knocked his forehead on the door jamb. Unable to resist the opportunity to sermonize, the Puritan suggested that "You are young, and have the world before you; stoop as you go through it, and you will miss many hard thumps." Franklin said he always remembered the older man's advice "when I see pride mortified, and misfortunes brought upon people by their carrying their heads too high."

They had some things in common. Besides a strong inclination toward moralizing, Mather, like his young visitor, had a head for science. Despite his backward notions regarding witchcraft, he'd been one of the first to experiment with inoculations to guard his fellow Bostonians against smallpox; Franklin later became a convert to the procedure after his son Francis succumbed to the disease. Mather and other Puritans also had a long tradition of self-governance in their churches— a democratic strain that would feed into broad support for the American Revolution among the clergy of New England. Yet in most respects, the two inhabited different epochs.

Franklin comes across as a man of our own era. Though he was almost forty years older than Thomas Jefferson and John Adams when the three sat down together to write the Declaration of Independence, he seems younger and a little more hip than either of the two. As biographer Walter Isaacson puts it, "Benjamin Franklin is the founding father who winks at us." George Washington seemed austere even to his contemporaries, usually addressed formally as "Your Excellency," although a few old soldiers called him "General." In contrast, the avuncular Franklin went by nicknames, just plain Ben or even, as Adams called him with rueful affection, "the Old Conjurer."

A lifelong tinkerer and inventor, Franklin would have been

equally amused and amazed at the cell phones and other gadgets that are so much a part of the early twenty-first century. No prude, he had a matter-of-fact attitude toward sexuality that would have made him right at home in these freewheeling times. Celebrated by his contemporaries as a revolutionary who "stole lightning from the skies and the scepter from tyrants," he wore his greatness with a casual air that never forgot its humble origins. He was equally comfortable with commoners and kings, less a man of the eighteenth century than a man for the ages.

The name Franklin came from a Middle English word that meant "freeman." The term applied to the middling classes that established themselves in the late Middle Ages, neither serfs nor titled aristocracy, but independent tradesmen and artisans who were able to acquire a bit of property and eventually a share of political power through their own native talent and their own hard toil. His distant ancestors were ardent Protestants, who during the Catholic reign of Queen Mary kept a banned English Bible tied to the underside of a stool, where it could be turned over one's lap and read aloud when the coast was clear, then instantly hidden if necessary. By Ben's times, the family's zeal had cooled considerably, however. Though Franklin claimed in his *Autobiography* that it was "a desire to exercise their religion with freedom" that drew his ancestors to America, economic motives also played a role. Wages were two or three times higher in the New World than in England, and Josiah Franklin, Ben's father, went to work in Boston as a tallow chandler, rendering animal fat into soap and candles—profitable enough to enable him to raise seventeen children, but still not lucrative enough to take all his sons into the family business.

The original plan was to educate young Benjamin for the ministry. He was enrolled at the Boston Latin School to prepare him for Harvard and eventual ordination. But either the cost of a Harvard degree proved too expensive, or more likely Josiah decided his son was insufficiently pious for his intended vocation. He may have noticed that young Ben found the long prayers at mealtime rather tedious, for example, for one fall day after his father had finished salting a barrel of provisions for the winter, his son had some practical advice. "I think, Father, if you were to say Grace over the whole cask—once for all—it would be a vast savings of time." Not long after, with only two years of formal schooling, it was decided that Benjamin should go to work as an apprentice with his older brother James, who had set up shop as a printer.

Ben had been given a chance to apprentice in other trades. With his father, he had walked through town, watching the silversmiths and barrel makers and cutlers grinding their knives to see which line of work he liked best, and Franklin never lost his sense of kinship with the laboring classes—people who could make things with their hands or knew how to use tools. He appreciated skilled workmanship. It appealed to his practical side and laid the groundwork for the technological innovations that later came out of his own home workshop— the first electrical battery, bifocal spectacles, and the Franklin stove. But young Benjamin settled on printing as a vocation, probably because of his love of books. Years later, a town in Massachusetts named itself after Franklin and asked him to donate a bell for the local church. The famous philanthropist told them to abandon the steeple and build a library instead, sending them "books instead of a bell, sense being preferable to sound."

An avid reader, Ben's exposure to a wide range of religious literature began to chip away at the beliefs he had absorbed as a youngster. "My parents had early given me religious impressions, and brought me through my childhood piously in the Dissenting way. But I was scarce fifteen, when, after doubting by turns of several points, as I found them disputed in the different books I read, I began to doubt of Revelation itself." The young man read even more books designed to quiet these qualms, but "It happened that they wrought an effect on me quite contrary to what was intended by them; for the arguments of the Deists, which were quoted to be refuted, appeared to me much stronger than the refutations; in short, I soon became a thorough Deist." It was the beginning of a lifelong venture to define his own beliefs, as opposed to having them defined by others.

Besides giving access to the written word, running a printing press gave Ben a chance to try his hand at composition, since printers in those days doubled as authors and journalists—not to mention pundits and publicists, caught up in all the fray of political debate. He taught himself to write, dissecting the works of essayists like Jonathan Swift and Joseph Addison, then trying his own hand on the same topic and learning from the results. Usually, he deemed his efforts poor in comparison with the originals. "But I sometimes had the pleasure of fancying that in certain particulars of small import I had been lucky enough to improve the method or the language, and this encouraged me to think that I might possibly in time come to be a tolerable English writer."

Not only was he tolerable. From his first appearances in print as Silence Dogood, writing as a sixteen-year-old boy under the assumed identity of a middle-aged matron, commenting in a gossipy way on the manners of her Massachusetts neighbors, on up through the 145 editions of *Poor Richard's Almanack* that appeared during his lifetime, Franklin became the most popular writer of his day, developing a wry, folksy style of humor that became an American trademark. "Fish and visitors stink in three days," was one of his adages. "Three can keep a secret if two of them are dead," was another. His wit could be sharp or lighthearted by turns. While Jonathan Edwards, his exact contemporary, was writing sermons on "Sinners in the Hands of an Angry God," Franklin was composing mock scientific articles on the intelligent design of the human elbow. Had the Almighty placed the joint farther down the forearm, or farther up, it would be so difficult to lift a wineglass to our lips! Clearly the Creator approved of tippling, Franklin concluded with tongue in cheek.

He could also laugh at himself. As a young man, Franklin remembered, he briefly flirted with vegetarianism, part of a rigorous regimen of self-improvement. His reasons for trying the diet were practical; when he didn't have to buy meat, he had more pocket money to purchase books, and the simple meals gave him extra time to study. Yet he also considered consuming animals a moral issue, "since none of them had or ever could do us any Injury that might justify the slaughter." Then on a sea voyage, he found himself becalmed with the other passengers. When the ship's crew began catching and frying cod, he was initially determined to stick by his principles. But the smell of frying fish made him reconsider. Then he remembered noticing, when the cod were being cleaned, smaller fish inside their stomachs, producing a happy thought: "If you eat one another, I don't see why we mayn't eat you." Himself a child of the Age of Reason, Franklin concluded the yarn with a wisecrack: "So convenient a thing it is to be a reasonable Creature, since it enables one to find or make a Reason for every thing one has a mind to do."

He made a lengthy list of virtues he wished to cultivate, from temperance to frugality and cleanliness, with a closing admonition to "Imitate Jesus and Socrates." But on the list of self-improvement projects, churchgoing never held a high priority. During his early years in Philadelphia, he did subscribe to the Presbyterian church, which included an assortment of Baptists, Congregationalists, and other dissenters. Ben was urged by the minister to try coming to services on five successive Sundays, and with both an open mind and some self-reproach over his lackadaisical attendance, Franklin consented. But he found the pastor's sermons "were chiefly either polemic arguments or explications of the peculiar doctrines of our sect." What made them so "uninteresting and unedifying" was that "not a single moral principle was inculcated or enforced, their aim seeming rather to make us good Presbyterians than good citizens." Such doctrinal disputations left him chilled.

Later, the church called an assistant minister from England who was given to preaching on practical morality, and Franklin found these "most excellent discourses." When the new assistant began attracting an audience with the city's freethinkers, however, the Presbyterian synod put him on trial for heresy. In a scorching pamphlet of 1730, Franklin likened the proceedings to the Spanish Inquisition and compared the prosecutors to asses—animals that are both "grave and dull." But his more lasting reaction was to help found a new, nondenominational religious organization in Philadelphia where preachers unwelcome in other churches could find a hearing. As Franklin wrote in his *Autobiography*, "If the Mufti of Constantinople were to send a missionary to preach Mahometanism to us, he would find a pulpit at his service."

He did believe that religious observance had a salutary effect on manners and morals, and Franklin financially supported the construction of new churches in the colonies. "As our province increased in people, and new places of worship were continually wanted, and generally erected by voluntary contribution, my mite for such purpose, whatever might be the sect, was never refused," he boasted. But churches ought to focus on what he considered the essentials of faith—the existence of the deity, the immortality of the soul, and charity toward one's neighbor. While honoring all denominations, he regarded them "with different degrees of respect, as I found them more or less mixed with other articles, which, without any tendency to inspire, promote, or confirm morality, served principally to divide us, and make us unfriendly to one another."

While Sabbath observance was never a priority—he used Sunday for reading and research—he did strongly encourage his daughter to attend Anglican services. "Go constantly to church, whoever preaches," he advised. "The act of devotion in the Common Prayer Book is your principal business there, and, if properly attended to, will do more towards amending the heart than sermons generally can do." Franklin respected the liturgy of the Church of England for its stately ritual, while at the same time wishing the worship service could be shortened and updated. That was behind his own attempt to edit and revise the Prayer Book, including the Lord's Prayer, which he rendered as follows:

> Heavenly Father, may all revere thee, and become thy dutiful children and faithful subjects. May thy laws be obeyed

on earth, as perfectly as they are in heaven. Provide for us this day, as thou has hitherto daily done. Forgive us our trespasses, and enable us to forgive those who offend us. Keep us out of temptation, and deliver us from evil.

It took daring to modify the words of Jesus. But Franklin considered his version "more concise, and better modern English."

When he attended church himself, his preferences varied. In 1774, he was present at the founding of the Essex Street Chapel, London's first Unitarian congregation. And in Britain he frequently attended the services of his friend and fellow scientist the Reverend Joseph Priestley (1733–1804). Priestley, who is credited with discovering oxygen, carbon monoxide, and hydrochloric acid in the course of his investigations, had briefly experimented with electricity like Franklin before turning his attention to chemistry, and it was Priestley who first recorded the famous story of Franklin flying a kite in a thunderstorm.

Historian Henry Steele Commager likens him to an English version of the venerable Franklin, "bustling about in science, politics, and education, full of benevolence and wisdom, ardent for freedom, confident of progress, the most practical of philosophers." Like his American counterpart, Priestley was an inventor: he puttered with a copying machine, made improvements to fire engines, and even discovered that India rubber could be used as an eraser. The two were associated through the Lunar Society, in Birmingham, where Franklin was a frequent guest of the "Lunatics"—so called because they met on the Monday nearest the full moon. All the members— including James Watt, of steam engine fame—shared a passion for science. As Erasmus Darwin, grandfather of the great biologist, described the gatherings, "what inventions, what wit, what rhetoric, metaphysical, mechanical, and pyrotechnical, will be on the wing, bandied like a shuttlecock from one to another of your troop of philosophers!"

Priestley's faith was a mix of old and new. He denied the supernatural inspiration of the scriptures and insisted the Bible be evaluated dispassionately, like any other historical document. While rejecting some passages as legendary, like the shepherds and the virgin birth, miracles such as the resurrection he accepted as authentic because attested by multiple witnesses (which was seemingly solid evidence in an era before scholars realized the gospels were written decades after the events they purportedly describe). During his years in Birmingham, Priestley published two of his major theological treatises, *A History of the Corruptions of Christianity* and *A History of the Early Opinions Concerning Jesus Christ*, both of which challenged the traditional doctrine of the Trinity. Like other Unitarians of the eighteenth century, Priestley objected to the dogma of God in three persons not so much because it was unscriptural—although that argument was made—but because the church's insistence on such doctrines detracted from the pragmatic tenor of Christ's teaching. Changing lives, not theological speculation, was at the heart of the gospel, and though Jesus was not to be worshiped in his own right, his loving example and message showed humankind a way toward oneness with God and neighbor.

These were incendiary opinions. And when his church, laboratory, and books were torched by mobs outraged at his religious and political heresies—for he was a vocal supporter of both the American and French revolutions—Priestley emigrated to Franklin's home city of Philadelphia in 1794. John Adams was among the founders who worshiped at the chapel he founded there; and had Franklin still been living, he would no doubt also have been present.

The Unitarians' rational approach to religion appealed to his intellect, yet Franklin was broad-minded enough to visit the camp meetings of the English revivalist George White-field (1714–70) as well. Whitefield was a sensational orator who could supposedly dissolve his listeners to tears simply by pronouncing the word "Mesopotamia." Prepared to resist the preacher's blandishments, Franklin found himself melting under the spell of emotion when the collection plate was passed:

> I had in my pocket a handful of copper money, three or four silver dollars and five pistoles in gold. As he proceeded I began to soften, and concluded to give the coppers. Another stroke of his oratory made me ashamed of that, and determined me to give the silver; and he finished so admirably, that I emptied my pocket wholly in the collector's dish, gold and all.

Despite their theological differences, the two men grew to like each other immensely. Once when Whitefield wrote the American that he was planning a trip to Philadelphia and had nowhere to lodge, Franklin offered his own home. The preacher responded politely that if the hospitality were extended "for Christ's sake," his host "should not miss of a reward." "Don't be mistaken," came Ben's rejoinder, "it was not for Christ's sake, but for your sake." Franklin recalled that "He used, indeed, sometimes to pray for my conversion, but never had the satisfaction of believing his prayers were heard."

He himself was not averse to formal prayers. When the Constitutional Convention seemed close to breaking down into bickering in 1787, an elderly Franklin restored civility and gave a sense of gravitas to the gathering by invoking the "Father of Lights" to illuminate the proceedings. He said to the assembled delegates:

> I have lived, Sir, a long time, and the longer I live, the more convincing proofs I see of this truth—that God governs in the affairs of men. And if a sparrow cannot fall to the ground without his notice, is it probable that an empire can rise without his aid? We have been assured, Sir, in the sacred writings, that "except the Lord builds the House they labour in vain that build it." I firmly believe this; and I also believe that without his concurring aid we shall succeed in this political building no better than the Builders of Babel: We shall be divided by our little partial local interests; our projects will be confounded, and we ourselves shall become a reproach and bye word down to future ages.

The senior statesman's motion to start each day's proceeding with a prayer was rejected by the Convention. Alexander Hamilton (1755–1804) quipped that the assembly didn't need any "foreign aid." But the delegates were so startled by the pious suggestion from the old rogue that they began to behave more creditably, recalled to their better selves. And that was perhaps Franklin's intention. He always believed that God was better served by good works than by any amount of intercessions or incantations. His was a practical creed and a simple one.

In a letter to the Reverend Ezra Stiles of Yale near the end of his life, Franklin stated that "I believe in one God, Creator of the Universe. That he governs it by his providence. That he ought to be worshiped. That the most acceptable service we render to him is doing good to his other children." These tenets he felt were essential to all religions; everything else was optional. As to Jesus, he commented:

> I think the system of morals and his religion, as he left them to us, the best the world ever saw or is likely to see; but I apprehend it has received various corrupting changes, and I have, with most of the present dissenters in England, some doubts as to his divinity, though it is a question I do not dogmatize upon, having never studied it, and think it needless to busy myself with it now, when I expect soon an opportunity of knowing the truth with less trouble.

If others wanted to believe that Jesus was the Son of God, Franklin had no objection, particularly if it had the effect of making his teachings better respected.

He gave a fuller accounting of his faith in a document titled "Articles of Belief and Acts of Religion," which he wrote as a young man in 1728. There he speculated that our solar system is only one among an infinitude of stars and planets, in a universe populated with a range of beings both inferior and superior to humankind—including a multiplicity of gods:

> When I stretch my Imagination thro' and beyond our System of Planets, beyond the visible fix'd Stars themselves, into that Space that is every Way infinite, and conceive it fill'd with Suns like ours, each with a Chorus of Worlds for ever moving round him, then this little Ball on which we move, seems, even in my narrow Imagination, to be almost Nothing, and my self less than nothing, and of no sort of Consequence.

There must be a supremely wise and powerful Being who has created this vast system and even the divinities themselves, Franklin held. "When I think thus, I imagine it a great Vanity in me to suppose that the *Supremely Perfect* does in the least regard such an inconsiderable Nothing as Man." Franklin could not conceive that this "Infinite Father," so far beyond our comprehension, expects or requires praise from such poor creatures as ourselves. Yet feeling also that people have a natural impulse to worship, "I think it seems required of me, and my Duty as a Man, to pay Divine Regards to SOMETHING." The being to whom Franklin paid homage was whatever "particular wise and good God" had devised our small corner of the cosmos. This being was far below the "Infinite," yet more approachable as a result and perhaps more prone to consider human petitions. The "Articles of Belief" conclude with a series of prayers composed for private devotion:

> For Peace and Liberty, for Food and Raiment, for Corn and Wine, And Milk, and every kind of Healthful Nourishment,
> *Good God I Thank thee.*
> For the Common Benefits of Air and Light, for useful Fire and delicious Water,
> *Good God I Thank thee.*
> For Knowledge and Literature and every useful Art; for my Friends and their Prosperity, and for the fewness of my Enemies,
> *Good God I Thank Thee.*
> For all thy innumerable Benefits; For Life and Reason, and the Use of Speech, for Health and Joy and every Pleasant House,
> *My Good God, I Thank thee.*

None of it makes reference to the Bible or Jesus, and Franklin's tone is tentative throughout. The "Articles of Belief" are filled with sentences that begin "I conceive," "I think it seems," and "It may be."

This was in keeping with a resolution made early in life to "forbear all direct contradiction to the sentiments of others, and all positive assertion of my own." A friend had told him that he was lacking in humility and, on self-examination, Franklin decided the criticism might be true. Afterwards, he avoided "language that imported a fixed opinion, such as certainly, undoubtedly, etc." and he began to use more modest circumlocutions such as "I conceive, I apprehend, or I imagine a thing to be so or so; or it so appears to me at present." Conversations went more smoothly after he discontinued the use of "dogmatical expression," he discovered, and his ideas found a readier reception among his listeners. But the uncertain tone in the "Articles of Belief" is probably real rather than feigned or adopted. Speculations about multiple worlds and many gods seem to have been youthful thought experiments; his later formulations of belief tended to be simpler and more down-to-earth. "The great uncertainty I found in metaphysical reasonings disgusted me, and I quitted that kind of reading and study for others more satisfactory."

He was little interested in otherworldly mysteries when there were so many more fascinating questions to be answered here on earth. As a young man, on his first trip across the Atlantic at the age of twenty, he had studied the behavior of dolphins and calculated the ship's position using a lunar eclipse. He also made medical investigations and was one of the first to suggest that flu "may possibly be spread by contagion," anticipating the germ theory of disease. He can fairly be credited with founding the science of weather prediction, being the first to theorize that warm air rising in the south might create low-pressure systems drawing winds from the north. Other minor researches ranged from charting the Gulf Stream to figuring the orbit of comets.

But of course it is for his discoveries regarding electricity that he is best remembered. Up until then, electricity had been thought to involve two types of fluids, vitreous and resinous. But Franklin unified the understanding of electrical phenomena, suggesting it could better be analyzed in terms of positive and negative charge, famously suggesting that lightning was no different from the flashing sparks that experimenters were beginning to generate by rubbing glass tubes in their laboratories. It was an enormous breakthrough.

Thunderbolts had plagued humankind time out of mind, and lightning was generally considered an expression of divine displeasure. In an Election Day sermon from 1696, Cotton Mather assured his listeners that the Almighty would "scatter our Enemies with His Hot Thunderbolts, and Thunder them into Ruine for ever." Church bells pealed at the approach of clouds to placate God's wrath, but the tolling wasn't at all effective. Belfries were blasted on a regular basis and bell-ringers were electrocuted by the hundreds over the course of Franklin's lifetime. "The lightening seems to strike steeples of choice and at the very time the bells are ringing," Franklin noted, "yet still they continue to bless the new bells and jangle the old ones whenever it thunders. One would think it was now time to try some other trick."

Even when the "Franklin rod" had proven its utility, some clergy were not convinced. The Reverend Thomas Prince, the minister of Boston's Old South Church, noticed that an earthquake occurred in 1755, after several of the devices had been installed around the city. In a sermon titled "Earthquakes the Work of God," he suggested that the Almighty's will could not be thwarted, not even by the "sagacious Mr. Franklin." The homily was not quite as backward as it sounds, but theorized that drawing the "electrical fluids" out of the skies might lead to a build-up of charged forces in the ground, resulting in tremors.

Others objected to the devices on theological grounds. "I have heard some Persons of the highest Rank among us, say, that they really thought the Erection of Iron Points, was an impious attempt to rob the almighty of his Thunder, to wrest the Bolt of Vengeance out of his hand," scoffed John Adams. Fortunately, the rods continued to proliferate, despite the clergy's misgivings.

Franklin never patented the lightning rod, nor did he expect to profit from any of his other creations. "As we enjoy great advantages from the invention of others, we should be glad of an opportunity to serve others by any invention of ours," he said sincerely. It was a sentiment in keeping with a long career of public service. The good that people can do singly is small in comparison to what they can do collectively, he always held. And so his greatest achievements were in organizing disparate individuals around a common purpose. Early on, he helped to establish the first circulating library in the New World. Not long after, he founded the University of Pennsylvania, the first nonsectarian institution of higher learning in America. He organized fire brigades and plans for lighting the city streets right down to the design of street lamps that would be cheap and easy to maintain. A better streetlight might be a small convenience, he granted, but it was often through such little increments that human happiness progressed.

Good government was not least among the improvements that made for human felicity. And the better part of Franklin's life was spent in statecraft. Thanks to his up-by-the-bootstraps background, he was among the most egalitarian and least elitist of America's founders. He seldom wore the powdered wigs that were the fashion among highborn gentlemen, preferring instead the rustic fur cap of the backwoodsman. When his daughter, Sally, sent him a newspaper clipping about the Order of the Cincinnati, a heredity title for officers of the American Revolution to be passed on to their descendants, Franklin ridiculed the idea. He favored direct elections, and by the end of his life had become a fierce opponent of slavery; his last public act was sponsoring a petition to Congress calling for abolition. He believed excessive wealth ought to be heavily taxed and put to work for the common good; a man had right to whatever possessions were necessary for his own maintenance, but beyond that, "all Property superfluous to such purposes is the Property of the Publick." Though he did as much as any man to gain the nation's independence by winning French support at the crucial moment, he regarded his role in brokering an end to the conflict with Britain as even more important, coining a phrase when he wrote that "there never was a good war or a bad peace."

He was a mediator, adept in the arts of reconciliation, a master of compromise, able to use charm and flattery to bring antagonists together to parley. For that, some called him a manipulator. But it was a style he had cultivated since his youth. Achieving his aims by indirection, he found, was the way to get things done.

He accomplished more than most men during his eighty-four years on earth. And though his faith in eternity might have seemed nebulous to some, it was enough to bring him comfort. Would a Creator bother to manufacture minds like Franklin's and millions of others, only to destroy them in the end? Not a very rational way to run a universe. More reasonable to suppose that "I shall, in some Shape or other, always exist." So when his final illness struck, he was ready to depart. His daughter expressed the dutiful hope that he might recover and live many more years, but Franklin calmly replied, "I hope not," and his wish was quickly granted, his children and grandchildren nearby.

As a young man of little more than twenty-one, when he was just starting out in the world, Franklin had written his own epitaph. The words reflected the mixture of amusement and irony with which he approached most matters of faith:

<blockquote>
The body of
B. Franklin, Printer;
(Like the cover of an old book,
Its contents worn out,
and stripped of its lettering and gilding)
Lies here, food for worms.
But the work shall not be lost:
For it will, (as he believed) appear once more,
In a new and more elegant edition,
Revised and corrected
By the Author.
</blockquote>

But while Franklin acknowledged his divine author, he was also very much the author of his own life. Among his many inventions, the most amazing was himself. He was a first edition, an American original.

5.

To Bigotry No Sanction

The Faith of George Washington

If Benjamin Franklin towered over others mentally, George Washington was another kind of titan, and the larger-than-life awe in which he was held by contemporaries may have been partly due to his gargantuan stature. At a time when the average American male was just five feet six inches in height, Washington was a big man, about six feet four inches tall, weighing in at just over 200 pounds when he had Martha's kitchen to sustain him, but dropping to a wiry 175 pounds when ranging through the Allegheny wilderness or on limited rations with his men.

A champion wrestler, he could still throw contenders half his age when commanding the armies of the republic. And while he never tossed a silver dollar across the Potomac, he did claim to be able to fling a stone farther than anyone he'd ever met. In addition to all this, he was an outstanding equestrian who in one battle had five mounts shot out from under him, managing repeatedly amid the confusion of combat to snag a new steed from among those who had lost their riders. Thomas Jefferson called him the best horseman of his day. In short, he was a superb physical specimen. Dressed in all his finery—for Washington was a clothes hound who liked to be fashionably attired whether the garb was military or civilian, and he was the only one among the delegates to the first Continental Congress to wear a blue-and-buff colonel's uniform—he cut a dashing figure.

Women found him captivating. "Dignity with ease and complacency, the gentleman and the soldier look agreeably blended in him," swooned Abigail Adams. "Modesty marks every line and feature of his face." And the slightly smitten lady was reminded of these lines by Dryden:

> Mark his majestic fabric; he's a temple
> Sacred by birth, and built by hands divine;
> His soul's the deity that lodges there;
> Nor is the pile unworthy of the god.

"He had so much martial dignity in his deportment that there is not a king in Europe but would look like a valet de chambre by his side," confirmed Dr. Benjamin Rush.

Washington's was a lordly bearing, but it was the inner man, not the outer, that seemed most impressive. He was quiet, not given to boasting (except about his pitching arm), and his words were well chosen, calculated for maximum effect. A colleague in Virginia's House of Burgesses observed, "He is a modest man but sensible and speaks little—in action cool, like a bishop at his prayers." Later in life, Washington advised a nephew to "make yourself *perfectly* the master of your subject" before speaking in public. "Never exceed a *decent* warmth, and submit your sentiments with diffidence." Calm in crisis and in careful control of his own emotions, Washington exuded steadiness and considered judgment—a man others might turn to when the fighting started.

The air of competence and command that he carried was acquired, not inherited, the product of long years of learning and hard work. Like Franklin, he was mostly self-taught, for the boy's hopes of studying in England ended at age eleven, when his father died. Augustine Washington had belonged to the middling level of Virginia planters; the modest home where George lived with his four younger siblings and two older half brothers had just six rooms. An inventory listed the family's possessions: one plated soupspoon and a small variety of other silver, but most of the household utensils were whittled of wood. The terms of his father's will promised to leave George with a working small farm of 260 acres (and ten slaves), along with a larger tract of undeveloped backcountry, when he reached his majority, but Lawrence and Austin, sons of his father's first wife, received the bulk of the estate. From an early age, George realized that his fortune would have to be self-made.

He applied himself to his studies with determination, and character education formed an important part of the curriculum. Lesson books preserved from his childhood contain 110 maxims for how a gentleman should comport himself, copied from a Jesuit-inspired sixteenth-century handbook of etiquette titled *Rules of Civility and Decent Behavior*. Some, like Rule 9, stressed good manners: "Spit not in the fire." Others involved table etiquette: "Cleanse not your teeth with the table cloth, napkin, fork or knife, but if others do it let it be done wt. A Pick Tooth." But many more gave moral counsel, like "Rule 17: Be no flatterer" and "Rule 56: Associate yourself with men of good quality if you esteem your reputation, for 'tis better to be alone than in bad company." The last rule was to keep alive the "spark of celestial fire called conscience." All were exhortations the youth took to heart, and his personal code of conduct became more important than any official creed; as biographer Willard Sterne Randall remarks, "Washington practiced these rules more closely than the precepts of any religion."

There was nothing ascetic about his makeup. As much as most men of his background, Washington enjoyed a boisterous party and going to the theater, along with gambling and drinking in moderation. Yet there was a streak of Stoicism in his nature, and among classical philosophers, he was especially fond of Seneca. "It is a rough road that leads to the heights of greatness," wrote this first-century Roman, words that Washington must have pondered more than once as he built highways through the wilderness foot by rugged foot over the Cumberland Gap during the French and Indian War, fighting mud and mosquitoes as much as dodging bullets.

The bullets never seemed to hit, anyway. He wrote his brother Jack that he found "something charming in the sound" of musket balls whistling through the air, and though they often pierced his clothing, the projectiles never scratched him. Washington ascribed his good fortune to Providence (a term he used frequently) and to "the uncertainty of human things." Washington knew how chance and fortune could disrupt the best-laid strategies; he did not believe in an entirely tidy universe. And while his "Providence" sounded like the kind of higher power that might answer prayers, he also spoke of the governing power behind events as a stern necessity, impervious to supplication. "There is a Destiny, which has the Sovereign control of our Action," he wrote to Sally Fairfax, "not to be resisted through the strongest efforts of Human Nature." Bullets might hit or miss, but the mishaps of battle, like other tragedies, were beyond prevention. Was this faith or fatalism at work, or perhaps a mixture of both?

Whatever it was, it made him a bit reckless of danger, giving him "resolution to Face what any Man durst." Though he subsequently claimed to want nothing more than the life of a country squire, his path took him away from Mount Vernon for years together and frequently into harm's way. From an early age, Washington chose a military career—one that promised honor but also risk and hardship.

Washington nearly joined the navy—and history might have taken a different turn had he been accepted as a midshipman in His Majesty's fleet rather than becoming the commander of a colonial regiment—but his mother vetoed the move. Mary Ball Washington seems to have been a controlling and possessive parent, and while her son was always proper, there was little affection in their relationship. His letters typically began with the salutation, "Honored Madam," and he signed off, "Your Dutiful Son."

When the old woman died, George told his sister Betty that he had taken his final leave of their mother in Fredericksburg, "never expecting to see her more." There was no mention of meeting in the hereafter, and indeed Washington's letters, including many notes of condolence written over the course of his lifetime, evince little expectation of loved ones being rejoined in heaven. Though he gave credence to a "World of Spirits," Washington's ruminations on death tended to stress separation more than continuity. Death was "that country from whence no Traveler returns," a land of shades and shadows. When Jack died, George spoke of his brother's departure as an "eternal farewell." Spending eternity with his mother probably wasn't wanted in any case. And it may have been partly to escape Mary Ball's unwanted dominance that George applied himself to studies that would take him far from home.

At age sixteen, he received his first job as a surveyor, mapping out the hinterlands of the Shenandoah Valley, where few Europeans had ever ventured. His very first lesson in bush survival, it was also a technical achievement that demonstrated an unusual aptitude for science and math. Notebooks from his early teens indicate that Washington was being tutored in geometry and trigonometry, carrying out physics experiments, calculating decimals and square roots, and learning how to measure the volumes of liquid and solids in a variety of containers. He was also being trained in use of the theodolite—the precision instrument surveyors need to measure vertical and horizontal angles and, by a process of triangulation, determine distances over rough terrain. "Practical surveying," Washington recorded, required "so much astronomy as is useful to a skilfull exercise . . . for discovering the latitude, meridians, &c.," along with a facility for computation. Though he never really learned to spell, by the age of thirteen or fourteen he had attained about the same level of proficiency in applied mathematics as a modern college graduate. Such knowledge would later prove useful, for engineering has always been an important weapon in the military's arsenal.

In civilian life, too, Washington had a decided scientific bent. His curiosity determined that there were 13,411,000 grains in a bushel of timothy. Wouldn't it be easier to cast the seeds automatically than by hand? At Mount Vernon, he devised a plow that automatically dropped seeds into the furrows as the blade broke loose the soil. Much later, as first president he would urge Congress to adopt a law protecting patents to encourage "the introduction of new and useful inventions," observing that "there is nothing which can better deserve your patronage than the promotion of Science." Though nowhere near an inventor of Franklin's ability, he was clever and mechanically minded. Always keen on labor-saving devices, he carried out time-and-motion studies that prefigured modern ergonomics, watching his workmen hew planks and carefully noting which steps might be eliminated. As president, he accompanied Thomas Jefferson to the outskirts of Philadelphia to study a threshing machine of novel design, corresponding with his secretary of state as well on the technical challenges of a canal connecting the Ohio and Potomac rivers. Another experiment on his own estate involved sowing wheat, oats, and barley at standard depths in carefully controlled environments—soils containing varieties of clay, manure, sand, and silt—to learn how differing composts affected the plants' growth. While he was eager to learn from others, devouring textbooks on horticulture, he also liked to find out for himself. Naturally, he gravitated to others who were similarly inclined.

At age twenty, George Washington joined the Freemasons, a semi-secret society with scientific leanings that eventually attracted many other leaders of the American Revolution, including thirteen who would sign the Declaration of Independence. Initiated as an Entered Apprentice in the fall of 1752, Washington took the rites of the order seriously. He eventually rose to become the highest-ranking Mason in the United States, "persuaded that a just application of the principles on which the Masonic order is founded must be promotive of private virtue and public prosperity," as he told his lodge mates after more than thirty years of ascending within the fraternity. Because the Masons had distinct spiritual overtones, Washington's association with them is worth exploring.

Freemasonry as the founders knew it was part philosophical society, part social improvement club, part mystic brotherhood. It had its beginning in 1717 with the organization of the Grand Lodge in London. Earlier Masonic lodges were composed mostly of stone workers, remnants of the craft guilds that built the great medieval cathedrals. But by the opening of the eighteenth century, these guilds were in decay. The Grand Lodge revived masonry by drawing in an entirely new breed of participants—called "speculative" masons—whose interests were mainly scientific and philosophical. Like their predecessors, these newcomers evinced an enthusiasm for architecture and engineering. Not content to carve in stone, however, "speculative" masons hoped to lay the foundations for an entirely new society.

John Desaguliers, whose Huguenot family brought him to England shortly after his birth in 1683, was among the principal founders of the lodge where these ideas germinated. As chair of Experimental Philosophy at Oxford, he was an intimate of Newton (who became godfather of Desaguliers's third son) and was named Curator and Demonstrator of the Royal Society. His great gift was as a popularizer. He was able to lecture freely on gravity, optics, geometry, and mechanics and, with the aid of ingenious working models, bring the concepts of elementary physics within reach of nonscholars. With the reinvention of Masonry, he was also able to popularize his religious viewpoints and give them an influence that would become worldwide.

An ordained deacon in the Church of England, he became the proponent for a faith whose God owed more to the ideals of the Enlightenment than to traditional Christian scriptures. For deity should be demonstrable, Desaguliers argued, like the laws of science, which his own work had proven to be within the grasp of even average minds. So theology should look to nature rather than to revelation for inspiration—to the vastness of Creation and the orderly working of its laws. And just as Newton was uncovering the existence of realities and relationships in the natural world that seemed beyond dispute, a purely natural religion might avoid the disputations that had so vexed human history. Persecutions of the kind that drove his own family from France would become a thing of the past if only people would reorient their faith, away from doctrinal differences and variant readings of the Bible, toward what seemed to Desaguliers to be beyond question—the existence of God (whom he called the Great Architect and Organizer of the World) and the unity of humankind.

These were ideas that resonated with other scientists, and in London at least a quarter of the newly established lodge were members of the Royal Society. They elected Desaguliers Grand Master in 1719, and masonry began to grow. By 1722 there was a lodge in Ghent, and four years later another appeared in Paris. In 1731—the year that saw the institution of America's first lodge—one was also founded in Russia. Bringing together lords and commoners, the lodges fostered a degree of social mixing, where brothers might "meet upon the level." A global network was forming that, despite local variations, subscribed everywhere to the Constitution of the Freemasons that Desaguliers helped to craft.

While the manuals of the older Masonic societies, dating from the Middle Ages, all made reference to the Trinity, the new Masonic Constitution was silent on this point and never mentioned Christ. In a paragraph on "God and Religion," the Constitution enjoined newly minted Masons to overcome their theological differences to join in common moral endeavor:

> But though in ancient times Masons were charg'd in every Country to be of the Religion of that Country of Nation, whatever it was, yet 'tis now thought more expedient only to oblige them to that Religion in which all Men agree, leaving their particular Opinions to themselves, that is to be *good Men and true*, or Men of Honour and Honesty, by whatever Denominations or Persuasions they may be distinguished. . . .

The "religion in which all Men agree" could clearly not be Roman Catholicism or any of the varieties of Protestantism where disagreements were so prominent. By definition, it had to be more universal than that, and many Masons hoped that their movement would provide a groundwork for a unifying world faith: international in scope, ethical in outlook, and naturalistic in spiritual orientation.

Early American Masons included men like John Hancock and Paul Revere, Alexander Hamilton and John Marshall, Ethan Allen, Thomas Paine, and Benjamin Franklin, who was the first to publish the Freemason's Constitution in America and who designed Philadelphia's Masonic lodge. But Washington, who took his presidential oath of office on a Masonic Bible and laid the cornerstone of the nation's Capitol building with a Masonic trowel, was preeminent among them. Though he still occasionally attended worship in the Anglican tradition into which he had been born, and even helped to build the Pohick Anglican Church near Mount Vernon, he began to avoid the use of the word "God" in his private letters and public statements, resorting instead to Masonic circumlocutions like the Almighty, All-Wise Disposer of Events, Grand Architect of the Universe, or Beneficient Being (never Savior, Redeemer, or other Christological formulations).

Washington's church attendance began to dwindle after his initiation to Freemasonry, for he was growing increasingly impatient and bored by the discourses he heard there. In 1768, according to his diaries, he went to church on fifteen days and hunted foxes on forty-nine, as well as attending a horse race, three balls, two plays, and receiving at least one reprimand from a Scotch Presbyterian friend for spending too much time playing cards. In January of the following year he hunted twelve days and went to church once. Sabbath attendance may not be a very precise measure of religious fervor in any case, since divine services in the eighteenth century were opportunities to flirt, network, and gossip before and after worship. "Giving and receiving letters of business, reading Advertisements, consulting about the price of Tobacco, Grain &c. & settling either on the lineage, Age or qualities of favourite Horses" were subjects of many Sunday conversations. In all his diary entries where Washington noted going to church, he never alluded to the topic of the sermon or any spiritual reflections that occurred to him. That apparently wasn't how his mind worked.

One Sunday in November 1789, shortly after he had been elected president, Washington was almost arrested for not attending church. Delayed in New England and anxious to reach his destination in New York, he set out early in the morning. As he passed through the village of Ashford in Connecticut, he was intercepted by the tithing man, responsible for enforcing local ordinances that prohibited travel on the Lord's Day. Like it or not, even the nation's chief had to abide by the law, but Washington seemed peeved about being detained. The president's diary indicates he used the interlude to rest his horses, but he found the tavern where he was forced to cool his heels "not a good one" and the sermon of Mr. Pond, the parson of a nearby church, "very lame discourses."

What about the president's prayer life? Tourists making the trek to Valley Forge in Pennsylvania will find the first building they encounter after leaving the visitors' center is the handsome Washington Memorial Chapel, whose most prominent feature is a series of stained-glass windows, depicting the life of Christ on one side and the life of Washington on the other. Over the main entrance, according to the chapel's handout, is a scene of "Washington in prayer at Valley Forge," kneeling in the snow and calling on divine assistance for the beleaguered American cause. Why the general would have been kneeling on the cold, soggy ground is a puzzle, since Washington preferred to stand at prayer—even when warm and dry inside an Anglican church, where bending the knee is customary. The concocted incident has no basis in history and is entirely the work of the Episcopalian minister Mason Locke Weems, who published the first biography of George Washington in 1800 and invented the cherry tree episode as well as other "curious anecdotes" (as he called them) intended to clothe the Virginian's memory with an aura of saintliness. If Washington never told a lie, the same could not be said of Parson Weems, who never let the facts get in the way of a good story.

The truth is that Washington was never a communicant in the Anglican Church, and he made a special point of avoiding going to church when he knew that communion would be served. Martha Washington (1731–1802), who was more devout, invariably took the sacrament whenever it was available, making her husband's refusal even more noticeable. James Abercrombie, the rector of the church Washington attended during his residence in Philadelphia, publicly rebuked the president in a sermon for what he called "the unhappy tendency of example, particularly of those in elevated stations, who uniformly turned their backs upon the Lord's Supper." Scolding the president backfired, however. A United States senator told the rector of a dinner with Washington shortly after the reprimand, where the president related receiving on the preceding Sunday "a very just reproof from the pulpit for always leaving the church before the administration of the sacrament." Washington said that he

> honoured the preacher for his integrity and candour; that he had never sufficiently considered the influence of his example, and that he would not again give cause for the repetition of the reproof; and that, as he had never been a communicant, were he to become one then, it would be imputed to an ostentatious display of religious zeal, arising altogether from his elevated station.

Abercrombie complained that Washington "never afterward came on the morning of Sacrament Sunday, though, at other times, he was a constant attendant in the morning," and concluded by questioning the president's piety. "That Washington was a professing Christian, is evident from his regular attendance in our church," the rector fumed, "but sir, I cannot consider any man as a real Christian who uniformly disregards an ordinance so solemnly enjoined by the divine author of our holy religion."

Whether Washington qualified as a "real Christian" is an open question. He seldom mentioned Jesus. In a letter announcing the disbanding of the Continental Army in 1783, he did make a singular reference to "the Divine Author of our blessed religion" (notable because the phrase was so unusual for him), and in a speech to the Delaware chiefs, whose tribe had converted to Christianity some years earlier, he commended them upon their "wish to learn our arts and way of life, and above all, the religion of Jesus Christ." More often, he went to lengths to avoid such usage. Bishop William White, who was the brother of Mary Morris, one of Martha Washington's oldest and closest friends, wrote that "I do not believe that any degree of recollection will bring to my mind any fact which would prove General Washington to have been a believer in the Christian revelation." In the twenty volumes of Washington's collected correspondence, there is not one reference to Christ.

His interest in religion was mainly practical. As commanding officer, for instance, Washington enjoined his troops to conduct themselves as "Christian soldiers," just as he ordered them to refrain from swearing, drunkenness, and other habits ill-suited to army discipline. Being a Christian, in such cases, implied good conduct rather than personal conversion.

Appointing chaplains to the regiments was not surprising, either, at a time when some colonies still had church establishments, but Washington wanted the chaplains chosen by the men themselves, to reflect each regiment's own spiritual preferences. When Congress formulated a plan to appoint chaplains at the level of larger army units (brigades), Washington voiced his support for "a more generous toleration." He worried that brigade appointments would introduce religious disputes into the army and "compel men to a mode of worship they do not profess." Popular election of chaplains could be problematic, however. When the Rhode Island Regiment selected the Reverend John Murray to be their pastor, other clergy objected. Murray preached universal salvation—denying the doctrine that sinners would face everlasting punishment. Yet Washington was less concerned with theological correctness than with making sure the troops were satisfied. "General Orders, September 17th, 1775—The Rev. Mr. John Murray is appointed Chaplain to the Rhode Island Regiments, and is to be respected as such."

Like other revolutionary spirits, Washington may have harbored private doubts about the reality of heaven, hell, and other points of Christian doctrine that kept him from being a full communicant in the church, while still acknowledging the moral teachings that most denominations shared. It's hard to be sure, because he was reticent about his inmost beliefs. Bishop White recalled that "although I was often in the company of this great man, and had the honour of dining often at his table, I never heard any thing from him that could manifest his opinions on the subject of religion." Certainly he never broadcast his theology from the political rostrum. Maybe Washington simply took more seriously than most the words from the Sermon on the Mount, "Beware of practicing your piety before men."

Assuredly he took other admonitions from that sermon seriously—including the giving of alms. By all accounts, he was a generous man who contributed freely to charity. His position as a vestryman meant that he was responsible for administering the county's poor fund—for the vestry was more a civil office than an ecclesiastical one at that time—and when he left Mount Vernon to lead American forces in the Revolution, he gave detailed instructions to maintain the level of giving on his estate at forty to fifty pounds a year (roughly two thousand dollars in today's money), instructing his overseer, Lund Washington, a distant cousin, to "Let the Hospitality of the House, with respect to the poor, be kept up." Later, he subsidized old army chums with interest-free loans. When Thomas Nelson, a brigadier general from the Continental Army, passed away—leaving his widow and eleven children deep in debt after giving his entire fortune to the cause of independence—Washington did all he could, including appointing Nelson's son to his secretarial staff. At home, Washington's instructions were to provide food and shelter to anyone in need who came to the door. By these measures, the first president was generous but not lavish in good works.

Outwardly, he was careful to maintain the appearance of even-handedness, according all denominations the same measure of respect. At Mount Vernon, he was an equal opportunity employer, willing to hire "Mohometans, Jews, or Christians of any Sect, or they may be Atheists," so long as they were able workers. And when he did attend religious services, he was careful to make official visits to every sort of congregation, Quaker, Jewish, Methodist, and even (in his own words) "the

Presbyterian Meeting in the forenoon and Romish Church in the afternoon," recalling that during one visit to Pennsylvania he had attended worship at a Dutch Reformed church, "which, being in that language not a word of which I understood I was in no danger of becoming a proselyte to its religion by the eloquence of the Preacher."

As a religious pluralist, he deplored sectarian bickering: "Of all the animosities which have existed among mankind, those which are caused by differences of sentiments in religion appear to be the most inveterate and distressing, and ought most to be deprecated." Washington went to extra lengths to repair relations between Protestants and Catholics, a religious minority at the time often viewed with suspicion by other Americans. John Adams wrote an entire "Dissertation on the Canon and the Feudal Law" during the Stamp Act crisis, for instance, tracing the roots of American democracy to Luther's Reformation. Many saw Catholicism as a source of absolutism and the Vatican as hostile to liberty.

Burning the pope in effigy on November 5 had been an English custom since 1605, when a "Gunpowder Plot" to blow up the British Parliament ended in the executions of several Jesuit conspirators. But Washington forbad Guy Fawkes festivities among his soldiers because these antipapal bacchanals were likely to rankle his Catholic troops. He gave special orders to his officers to respect Catholic churches and the property of religious orders on an expedition into French Quebec. Of course, France was an important ally—officially Catholic in faith—and could not be offended without repercussions to the war effort. A strategic alliance had to be protected, but a vital principle was also at stake. "While we are contending for our own liberty, we should be very cautious of violating the rights of conscience in others," Washington warned, admonishing the troops not to insult the Indian nations of those regions, either.

In his public pronouncements he continually emphasized that America was founded on the precept of freedom of religion, which he called an "enlarged and liberal policy" the world would do well to emulate. To the Jewish congregation of Newport, Rhode Island, he offered assurances that the government of the United States "gives to bigotry no sanction, to persecution no assistance," requiring only that the adherents of differing faiths conduct themselves as good citizens. Significantly, Washington added that "it is now no more that toleration is spoken of," as if religious minorities were merely vexations to be endured by members of a more predominant faith. His vision for the nation went beyond tolerance to an active embrace of spiritual variety.

Washington was able for most of his career to bring cohesion to that variety, rallying Americans of varied backgrounds and beliefs around common aspirations. First as commander in chief of the Continental Army, then as presiding officer at the Constitutional Convention, and finally as the nation's first president, he inspired trust based on unshakeable integrity of character. He never took a salary for his eight years in uniform during the Revolution. To the amazement of monarchs in Europe, he relinquished power after defeating the mightiest empire on earth and retired to his farm as a private citizen. During the drafting of the Constitution, he let it be known that he would support any "tolerable compromise," seldom speaking except to insist that congressional districts be small enough to keep representation close to the people. He did not campaign for the presidency, and in the Electoral College received a unanimous vote—ascending to the highest office in the land by the country's nearly universal acclamation.

As president, however, even the irreproachable Washington came under fire from an electorate increasingly polarized over the French Revolution. At first, most Americans welcomed the birth of a new republic that seemed a sister to their own. Washington himself received the key to the Bastille, passed along from Thomas Paine and the Marquis de Lafayette, describing it as "the token of victory gained by liberty over despotism." But with the guillotining of the king and the outbreak of war between France and England, opinion shifted. Some saw Britain as the enemy—George III was once again trying to quash the people's rightful liberties. Others continued to revere English law, with its provisions for trial by jury and other checks on governmental power, as the cornerstone of America's own cherished freedoms.

Anything seemed possible in those tumultuous times, from the advent of a utopian society to the complete breakdown of civilization, and the mood was near hysterical. Jefferson and other friends of the French were labeled radicals, determined to undermine religion and uproot all authority, while the Federalists, including Washington and Adams, were attacked as supercilious and arrogant, lording it over the people. In simplest terms, the division was between those who believed that an excess of democracy could lead to anarchy and mob rule, versus those who believed there could never be such a thing as too much freedom ("My most earnest wish is to see the republican element of popular control pushed to the maximum of its practicable exercise," said Jefferson). As with the "culture wars" of more recent times, the atmosphere grew venomous. Political parties and factions were forming that threatened to split the new nation down the middle.

In his Farewell Address, Washington warned against the

factious spirit and urged his fellow citizens to reconcile their differences. Religious institutions had an important role to play in the healing, he believed. Churches and synagogues could help elevate men and women above narrow interests and partisan agendas. They could be sources of unity, overcoming animosity and pettiness. "Of all the dispositions and habits which lead to political prosperity, Religion and morality are indispensable supports," Washington said in his Farewell:

> In vain would that man claim the tribute of patriotism, who should labor to subvert these great pillars of human happiness, these firmest props of the duties of men and citizens. The mere politician, equally with the pious man, ought to respect and to cherish them. A volume could not trace all their connections with private and public felicity. Let it simply be asked: Where is the security for property, for reputation, for life, if the sense of religious obligation desert the oaths which are the instruments of investigation in courts of justice? And let us with caution indulge the supposition that morality can be maintained without religion. Whatever may be conceded to the influence of refined education on minds of peculiar structure, reason and experience both forbid us to expect that national morality can prevail in exclusion of religious principle.

Washington was convinced that faith had a crucial role to play in the newly founded republic. At its best, the religious impulse enabled people to lay aside private gain and personal advantage in favor of the common good. And while the cognoscenti might be able to base their ethics on purely rational principles, the average run of humanity needed the stimulus of religion to help them do the right thing. A hundred years earlier, John Locke had postulated that "the greatest part cannot *know*" and so "they must *believe*." Washington agreed. But for him *every* belief system had social utility—and theology was secondary to ethics.

Washington had been vilified in the newspapers. One New York editorial fulminated that "he holds levees like King, receives congratulations on his birthday like a King, employs his old enemies like a King, shuts himself up like King," conducting himself like a grandee. So it was fitting for the Farewell to be published as an article in the *American Daily Advertiser*, addressed directly from the president to the citizens who had elected him. By announcing his retirement in the popular press, Washington refuted the charge of royalism with the most powerful statement possible, establishing a precedent for limiting the presidency to two terms that would last until Franklin Roosevelt. Accused of aristocratic pretensions, his nobility was finally revealed, not in amassing power, but in his willingness to give it up.

Washington's own farewell came suddenly. On Thursday, the twelfth of December, 1799, he spent several hours making the rounds of Mount Vernon despite the fact that "the weather was very disagreeable, a constant fall of rain, snow and hail with a high wind." That evening he complained of a sore throat. Depending as usual on his stout constitution to carry him through, he braved the weather again the next morning, marking several trees to be felled. Friday evening, he was scarcely able to breathe, and by Saturday he was dying. His condition was probably epiglottitus, an acute inflammation of the airways. According to his personal friend and longtime secretary Tobias Lear, who was with him through the ordeal as he struggled for oxygen, "He suffered extremely."

Knowing the end was near, Washington uttered no prayers and asked for no priest to attend his bedside. There were no expressions of repentance, no requests for favorite psalms or other spiritual comforts. With some difficulty, he spoke. "I am going. I die hard," he told his doctors, "but am not afraid to go." Tobias Lear, who left a detailed account of that day, expressed the hope that he might meet his comrade once more in heaven—but he was too good a reporter to suggest that George Washington reciprocated the utterance. Like his much admired Seneca, who said that the brave man "can look death in the face without any trouble or surprise," the old soldier died with quiet fortitude.

According to the instructions he had left, he was buried four days later. Measured for his mahogany coffin, Washington was laid out at six feet three-and-a-half inches. A back injury in old age had probably taken something off his height.

But in death, his stature would only grow. For a young republic learning how people of divergent faiths might form a single body politic, he modeled courtesy and spiritual restraint. He emphasized what people had in common, rather than what divided them. "With slight shades of difference," he told his countrymen and -women in his Farewell, "you have the same religion, manners, habits, and political principles." All his life, he tried to build bridges among people of goodwill. Against those who played what is now called "identity politics," he emphasized his fellow citizens' shared identity as Americans and members within a larger family of nations. "Cultivate peace and harmony with all," he admonished. "Religion and morality enjoin this conduct." He was as large in his sympathies as he was magnanimous in his sense of duty—truly a giant of history.

6.

My Own Mind
Is My Own Church

———•••———

The Faith of Thomas Paine

Every revolution needs a publicist whose words pack
firepower, who can deploy paragraphs the way general-
als marshal armies. The American Revolution required men
of other talents, too—strategists like Washington to win the
battlefield and diplomats like Franklin to negotiate the peace.
Patience, moderation, and the ability to build consensus are
important skills for those who intend to launch a new nation.
But the war for independence was one of the first modern

conflicts where mobilizing public opinion proved even more important than mustering cannon. For this work, the publicist had better be inflammatory rather than temperate. His message must be explosive if it is to ignite the sleeping energies of the citizenry and kindle them to the white heat needed to take up arms.

Thomas Paine was the publicist of 1776, who supplied the initial spark that led to independence and war with Britain. Writing for the masses, he was hard-hitting and incisive, using down-to-earth language he tried to make as simple as the alphabet. Above all, he was never boring. "Some people can be reasoned into sense, and others must be shocked into it," he sallied. "Say a bold thing that will stagger them and they will begin to think." By the nature of the role he played, he was destined to be a controversial figure, whose writings could excite the passions of his countrymen.

Thomas Paine came from the little village of Thetford, England. In 1737, at the time of his birth, the town typified the class distinctions that ruled Britain everywhere. Of two thousand inhabitants, only thirty-one were eligible to vote for Parliament, whose members met in London, seventy-five miles to the southwest. Back then, you had to be a property holder or have an income of at least forty pounds a year to cast a ballot. Paine's family, like most others, didn't qualify.

Joseph, his father, had a small business making stays for lady's corsets. His clients would have been among the gentility—women whose fine gowns and artificially narrow waists made them ornaments for great lords like the local duke of Grafton. Even a minor duke or duchess could fetch an income of ten thousand pounds per annum in those days. In contrast, the corset shop might bring in thirty pounds a year—certainly better than a schoolteacher's salary of ten or a ploughman's of eight, but still not enough to elevate the family into the ranks of enfranchised citizens.

Paine's family was doubly disinherited for religious reasons. While his mother was an Anglican, his father—with a much larger influence on the growing boy—was a member of the Quakers. Founded by George Fox in the mid-seventeenth century, these much-despised gentlefolk were determined to restore Christianity to a more pristine form. Fox taught that all people—regardless of sex or race or accidents of birth—possessed a divine spark or inner light which put them on a level footing in the eyes of the Most High. And this indwelling spirit, more than the Bible, constituted God's reconciling presence in the world. No intermediaries—neither priests, nor rituals, nor sacraments, nor churches, which Fox derisively called "steeple-houses"—were needed for salvation. Every person, regardless of rank or station, could enjoy a direct relation with the Eternal.

These were subversive doctrines. Quakers refused to take oaths in court or doff their hats to magistrates. They condemned the slave trade and addressed both peers and commoners with a simple "thee" or "thou," acknowledging no earthly titles beyond brother and sister. As conscientious objectors who tried to live out Christ's mandate not to return evil for evil, they refused military service. During Fox's lifetime, thousands of his followers were imprisoned, flogged, and even executed for these tenets.

The situation changed in 1689, when Britain's Toleration Act granted Quakers and other nonconformists the right to worship in their own manner. But dissenting sects were still excluded from voting or holding public office, nor were their members permitted to attend the state universities at Oxford or Cambridge. This history of persecution gave many of the Friends a defiant, oppositional edge. Certainly it gave Thomas Paine a fighting spirit.

He would later mock the pretentious titles of kings—"the *Honourable* plunderer of his country, or the *Right Honourable* murderer of mankind." He was an upstart, and a natural rebelliousness led him to challenge the Friends' stricter teachings. Calling himself "a Quaker without all its follies," the hard-drinking rebel was never a teetotaler. Nor, though he remained sympathetic toward the Quakers all his life, was he a pacifist. What he retained of his childhood faith was a commitment to radical equality and a fierce antipathy to privilege.

As a youngster, he says, "it was my good fortune to have an exceedingly good moral education, and a tolerable stock of useful learning." Though he attended grammar school, he never learned Latin, which formed the core curriculum for social climbers. But the deficit never bothered him. He grew to believe the study of dead languages was a hindrance to most students, who should learn to think for themselves rather than trusting the authority of the ancients. Even as a child, he recalled, "the natural bent of my mind was to science," where more important discoveries were being made in his own generation than in the previous thousand years.

Inquisitive, he began to question traditional religious doctrines early on. Tom was only seven or eight years old when he heard a sermon on "Redemption by the Death of the Son of God," the doctrine of the Atonement. "Making God Almighty act like a passionate man, that killed his son when he could not revenge himself in any other way" seemed abhorrent to him, "and as I was sure a man would be hanged that did such a thing, I could not see for what purpose they preached such sermons." No doctrine can be entirely healthy, he concluded, that shocks the mind of a child.

Prospects at home were limited. His formal education ended at thirteen, when he became an apprentice in his father's shop. Before he was twenty, he had shipped out on the *King of Prussia*, a British privateer that gave him his first taste of naval combat (England and France were then engaged in the Seven Years' War), but one tour of enlistment was enough. He tried his hand at teaching school, then managed to gain appointment as a tax collector whose job was to collect internal duties levied on alcohol and domestic goods like salt and soap. Although "exciseman" was an official government position, it was more racket than legitimate occupation, notoriously poorly paid. Tax collectors had to scratch a living by whatever means possible, which frequently meant corruption. Paine was elected by his fellow excisemen to write up a petition seeking better wages and working conditions from Parliament—his first exercise in polemical writing.

Visiting London to present the petition, he attended a series of "philosophical" lectures ranging over the properties of pendulums, the composition of the atmosphere, and the behavior of comets. One of the presenters, Benjamin Martin, was a globe maker and collector of fossils, while the other, James Ferguson, specialized in astronomy. Warning against a purely mechanical view of the universe, together they introduced listeners to the· "Omnipotent Architect" who created the "Divine Geometry of Nature." In the company of these Deists, Tom also learned about a celebrity scientist named Benjamin Franklin residing nearby. For the future rabble-rouser, a universe of fresh ideas and new connections was opening up.

Broad-shouldered and brown-haired with a rather ruddy complexion and in the prime of life, Tom was able to arrange a meeting with the great American experimenter. The two men had much in common; both were self-educated, from humble origins. With a letter of introduction from Franklin to encourage him, and little to hold him back (Paine's first wife had died, and his second marriage dissolved for reasons that are unclear), he set sail for America in 1774.

Philadelphia, where he stepped ashore, was the largest city in the colonies. A center of culture and commerce, its cobbled streets were filled with storefronts selling goods from all over the world. Perhaps most striking, churches from at least eight different denominations could be found within a few blocks of each other. William Penn—a close friend of George Fox—had founded the colony that bears his name as a "holy experiment" welcoming a multitude of religious persuasions.

The City of Brotherly Love also presented a refreshing contrast to the social stratification the stay-maker's son knew in England. Although there were a few wealthy merchants among the city's thirty thousand inhabitants, it was primarily a collection of craftsmen, artisans, and shopkeepers. Literacy was widespread, poverty rare. "Nothing there recalled the miserable London hovels and other abominations of the English capital," Paine found. As a wordsmith for the newly founded *Pennsylvania Magazine,* a position he obtained with Franklin's help, Paine extolled the virtues of his newly adopted country, where anything seemed possible. Who would have imagined the lowly son of a corset maker would rise to the position of editor, someone whose opinions mattered? The hardships of the previous thirty-seven years seemed to melt away as an unexpected world of opportunity—as a journalist and commentator—was opening.

As a newcomer, Paine could see the new country's possibilities more clearly than longtime residents. Most Americans at that point still considered themselves loyal subjects of the English throne. Tension had been building between the mother country and the colonies for years—in the form of economic and political conflict, flaring out in protests like the Boston Tea Party, then in actual bloodshed, like the Boston Massacre and the battling in Lexington and Concord. Yet even after a Continental Army had been formed, many colonists hoped the marriage with Britain could be saved, through negotiated settlement. Separation was unthinkable.

Before a revolution could take place on the battlefield, one had to occur in the minds of ordinary Americans, convincing them that independence was not only plausible but imperative. Thomas Paine, perhaps more than any other man, effected that transformation. The title for his pamphlet *Common Sense* had been suggested by the author's friend Benjamin Rush, who advised him line-by-line on the composition. The finished product appeared in January 1776, and sold over 150,000 copies before the year was out, arguing the case for separation with resounding force. Washington called its arguments "unanswerable."

Paine's attack on monarchy was the most effective catalyst. Many colonists had still been hoping George III would defend their rights against the depredations of Parliament. Only two years earlier, Thomas Jefferson had complained of a "chain of parliamentary usurpation" in *A Summary View of the Rights of British America*, appealing to the Crown as "the only mediatory power between the several states and the British Empire." But Paine portrayed King George as merely "the chief among plunderers" and princes as the perennial enemies of the people.

The current monarch might descend from William the Conqueror—but so what? Take away the fancy heraldry and the Conqueror was just a "French bastard landing with an armed banditti" to occupy England without the natives' consent. Paine even invoked the biblical books of Judges and Samuel to prove that, far from being based in divine right, kingship was an aberration in God's plan:

> Near three thousand years passed away from the Mosaic account of the creation till the Jews under a national delusion requested a king. Till then their form of government (except in extraordinary cases, where the Almighty interposed) was a kind of republic administered by a judge and the elders of the tribes.

According to Dr. Rush, the effects of *Common Sense* "were sudden and extensive upon the American mind. It was read by public men, repeated in clubs, spouted in Schools, and in one instance, delivered from the pulpit instead of a sermon by a clergyman in Connecticut." Jefferson would make King George, not Parliament, the chief villain in the Declaration he was drafting, while John Adams remarked that "without the pen of the author of *Common Sense*, the sword of Washington would have been raised in vain."

Paine could wield a sword as well as a pen. He joined a military unit called the Associators and was posted as an aide-de-camp to General Nathanael Greene. In November 1776 he was stationed with Greene's forces on a hilltop in New Jersey overlooking the Hudson River when he saw the British army deliver its first crushing defeat to Washington's ragtag band of volunteers, where the American commander lost nearly half his troops from the New York area. With winter fast approaching and disaster looming, Paine began a series called *The Crisis*. "These are the times that try men's souls," he cried:

> The summer soldier and the sunshine patriot will, in this crisis, shrink from the service of their country; but he that stands it now, deserves the love and thanks of man and woman. Tyranny, like hell, is not easily conquered; yet we have this consolation with us, that the harder the conflict, the more glorious the triumph.

Washington ordered the essay read aloud to every one of his troops on Christmas day, 1776, just before boarding the boats that would take them across the Delaware. Paine's words worked their magic, boosting the army to a surprise victory over the Hessians at Trenton. In the next edition of *The Crisis*, the phrase "the United States of America" appeared for the very first time—an appellation that quickly caught on.

Paine continued to fight in word and deed throughout the long conflict, rallying spirits when morale was low. On April 18, 1783, Washington announced the war was finally won, and the following day—the anniversary of the battle of Lexington and Concord which had taken place eight bloody years earlier—Paine wrote the thirteenth in the *Crisis* series, declaring that "the times that tried men's souls are over—and the greatest and completest revolution the world ever knew, gloriously and happily accomplished."

The victory had millennial overtones. For the founding of an American republic, Paine felt sure, was part of a divine deliverance. In *Common Sense*, he'd seen a hint of Providence in the geographic gulf between colonists and the Crown. "Even the distance at which the Almighty hath placed England and America is a strong and natural proof that the authority of one over the other was never the design of Heaven." Separated by an ocean, the New World offered safe haven for those fleeing persecution and seeking spiritual freedom. Now Heaven's intentions were coming to fruition. America represented a fresh beginning, a chance to shed the hereditary evils of class distinction, snobbery, and economic caste (which he likened to original sin) and to start human society anew, on a basis of freedom and parity. "The birthday of a new world is at hand," Paine enthused. "A situation similar to the present hath not happened since the days of Noah until now." Revolution was the deluge that would cleanse the earth of elitism and bring a new dispensation of hope for the common run of humanity.

References to the Bible came naturally, for Paine was intimately acquainted with it and could quote long biblical passages from memory. But that doesn't mean he took the scriptures literally. Rather he regarded Holy Writ as "a history of the times of which it speaks," much of it primitive and outdated. Shortly after writing *Common Sense*, Paine recognized "the exceeding probability that a revolution in the system of government would be followed by a revolution in the system of religion."

All religions encouraged morality in some measure, and every faith contained some morsel of goodness, at least in the beginning, Paine held. God welcomes a variety of devotion, just like a loving parent. "If we suppose a large family of children, who, on any particular day, or any particular circumstance, made it a custom to present to their parent some token of their affection and gratitude, each of them would make a different offering, and most probably in a different manner." One might present their father with a small poem, another with a fragrant bouquet, and each gift would be received with pleasure. Likewise, the Creator is delighted with a diversity of worship, but most pleased with acts of justice and mercy. Thus, "every religion is good, that teaches man to be good."

But religion became problematical when it became entangled with the pomp and power of the state. Then, it too often engendered lies, pious frauds, and prejudice, instilling a sense of superiority and entitlement among its practitioners rather than humility or love. Ecclesiastical overseers tried to ensnare people's minds with ignorance and superstition, as surely as political overlords attempted to enslave their bodies. Both needed to be jettisoned for the revolution to be complete.

Most of Paine's writing on religion was done abroad. For despite the popular success of his literary output, the author was nearly penniless after the war for independence. All proceeds from the sale of *Common Sense* went to buy mittens for the troops. Everything from *The Crisis* was likewise donated to the cause. The state of New York offered him a home and small parcel of land in New Rochelle in recognition of his wartime service, while Congress allotted him a onetime stipend of three thousand dollars. A measure that James Madison brought forward in Virginia—to recompense the patriot for his labors—was defeated. Faced with mounting debts and the necessity of finding a regular income, Paine traveled to Europe in hope of selling an invention.

Like other revolutionary spirits, Thomas Paine cultivated an interest in science and technology. While on a visit to George Washington's residence in Rocky Hill, New Jersey, in the autumn of 1783, the two men had spent the better part of a day on a flat-bottomed scow, investigating an "inflammable air" (probably methane) released from the river when muck was disturbed off the bottom, and likewise he had first found Benjamin Franklin through a scientific club frequented by instrument makers and mathematicians. During the war, he experimented with methods for producing saltpeter—a key ingredient of gunpowder—in home laboratories, and fiddled with a flaming arrow designed to ignite enemy munitions. A planing machine and smokeless candle (most of the tapers made in America at that time gave off sooty fumes) were other gadgets from his workshop.

But his most serious piece of engineering was the design of an iron bridge that would arch over a long span of water without the need for supporting piers. He was inspired, he said, by the spider's web: "I naturally supposed that when nature enabled that insect to make a web she taught it the best method to put it together." Franklin was impressed with the scheme, but advised Paine (whom he called "my adopted political son") that he might have an easier time selling the novelty with an endorsement from the Royal Society of Britain or the French Academy of Sciences.

The design drew large crowds when exhibited in London and Paris. Shortly after his arrival in the French capital, the Academy declared in August of 1787 "that Mr. Paine's plan of an iron bridge is ingeniously imagined, that the construction of it is simple, solid and proper . . . and that it is deserving of a trial." Jefferson, who engaged the inventor in a lengthy exchange on railings, equilibrium, catenaries, and other technical details, praised the model as promising "to be cheaper by a great deal than stone, and to admit a much greater arch." But the bridge would never get built. The French Revolution erupted, and Paine's short trip to Europe extended into fifteen years as he was swept into the action, producing two of his greatest works in the process.

The Rights of Man was written in 1791 in direct response to Edmund Burke's *Reflections on the Revolution in France*, which had appeared the previous year. The authors were well acquainted. Burke had been an early supporter of the American colonies in their quest for independence. But a revolution across the sea was one thing, while one next door was far more alarming. For the rule of law was like a tree, Burke argued, a product of organic growth that could not be uprooted and replanted overnight, or redesigned according to abstract notions of popular sovereignty. "The very idea of the fabrication of a new government is enough to fill us with disgust and horror," he shivered. Especially threatening was the notion that "a king is but a man; a queen is but a woman." The demand that people should select their own governors was a delusive, dangerous notion. For the British, the comfort of being ruled by a hereditary monarch and hoary aristocracy felt like "a benefit, not a grievance."

Paine hit back with a ringing defense of "liberty, equality, and fraternity" that traced human brotherhood back to the beginning of the world. People are created in one kind and one degree—in the image of God—not only according to Genesis but to every other known religion, Paine contended. Whatever distinctions exist between kings and commoners must therefore be perversions of the divine intent. The idea of a hereditary monarch was as nonsensical as that of "an hereditary mathematician, or an hereditary wise man; as absurd as an hereditary poet laureate." Legitimate power is not inherited and never absolute, but granted conditionally by the people. Thus governments either grow *out* of the people's wishes or are imposed *over* them, by force or conniving. And because people everywhere are endowed by God with inalienable rights that include freedom of speech, opinion, conscience, and association, the best way to serve God is by serving others and extending those same rights to all.

The Rights of Man was banned in England and its author charged with seditious libel. Printers were harassed and brought to trial. Nonetheless, Paine's book managed to sell over two hundred thousand copies in Great Britain (Paine's own estimate was double that), with translations in France, Holland, Germany, and even far-off Transylvania, where it was rendered into Hungarian at the Unitarian college in Kolozsvár. Few books before had reached such a large audience.

In the United States, the volume created its own furor because of a printer's error. James Madison obtained a copy of the manuscript prior to its publication, which he passed on to Thomas Jefferson, with a request that he forward it to the pressman. Jefferson appended his own note to the printer, explaining why the manuscript was coming from him. He also wrote that he was pleased "something was at length to be publicly said against the political heresies which had of late sprung up among us, not doubting but that our citizens would rally again around the standard of *Common Sense*."

Inadvertently, his words were included as a foreword to the book. And the phrase "political heresies" was a not-so-veiled reference to the work of John Adams, inflaming what was already a growing ideological rift between the two men, chilling a previously warm relationship. Years later, through the mediation of their mutual friend Benjamin Rush, the two managed to reconcile. But in the meantime, Americans were increasingly fractured—friend against friend over the turmoil in Europe.

Paine had his own mixed feelings about the events in France. Driven from the land of his birth, he was welcomed as a hero across the Channel and elected to the National Convention, representing Calais. Like most Americans, Paine was favorably impressed with the early stages of the revolution. "Little inconveniences, the necessary consequence of pulling down and building up, may arise," he assured Dr. Rush. "But even these are much less than ought to have been expected." Paine actively participated in drafting the French Constitution of 1793. Then things unraveled.

Prosecuting the king was a turning point. Paine believed in deposing Louis XVI, but not beheading him. Send the monarch to America, he urged, where he might learn that "the true system of government consists not in kings, but fair, equal and honorable representation." But vengeance prevailed, and as the Terror commenced, the revolution turned on its own. Thousands were arrested, dozens guillotined each night. By the end of 1793, Paine found himself in the Luxembourg prison in Paris, wondering if he would be decapitated.

The publicist decided to pick up his pen. Years before, he had predicted a revolution in religion would eventually follow the events of 1776. Now such an upheaval was occurring. The Christian calendar in France was declared defunct. A Goddess of Reason had been installed in Notre Dame cathedral. Missals were being sold as paper to wrap fish and altar clothes turned into uniforms for the French infantry. With the cannon roaring across Europe, Tom Paine dropped his own bombshell.

The Age of Reason, begun during his imprisonment, ignited a firestorm, running through twenty-one reprints in the United States in the decade following its publication, engendering at least thirty-five counterattacks. Paine dismissed the Bible, which he considered a blend of poetry and hearsay. Those seeking knowledge of God should look to Creation rather than to the scriptures. "That which is now called natural philosophy, embracing the whole circle of science," he proclaimed, "is the true theology":

> Does not the creation, the universe we behold, preach to us the existence of an Almighty power, that governs and regulates the whole? And is not the evidence that this creation holds out to our senses infinitely stronger than any thing we can read in a book that any imposter might make and call the word of God?

The heavens were expanding during the eighteenth century, and like Franklin, Paine was impressed by the vastness of the starry realm and the likely existence of life elsewhere in the cosmos. Old ideas of God were being tested by the discovery of deep space.

The ancients, beginning with the Greeks and Ptolemy, on down to Copernicus had supposed the distance from the Earth to the Sun to be a mere five million miles. But data gathered during observations of the transit of Venus confirmed that our solar system was nearly a hundred times larger than the entire Ptolemaic universe. With the discovery of Uranus in 1781, the scale of the solar system doubled again. And beyond that? By midcentury, philosophers like Immanuel Kant had begun to speculate that the fuzzy patches of light stargazers were calling "nebulae" might themselves be "island universes" containing millions of suns like our own. "To believe that God created a plurality of worlds, at least as numerous as what we call stars, renders the Christian system of faith at once little and ridiculous," Paine reflected. Amid these myriad spheres, why would God have singled out one small planet, or the inhabitants of one earthly tribe, to favor with his special attention?

Belief in extraterrestrials was au courant during the Enlightenment. In 1698 the astronomer Christiaan Huygens, first to describe the rocky rings of Saturn, penned a treatise on *The Celestial Worlds Discover'd: or, Conjectures Concerning the Inhabitants, Plants and Productions of the World in the Planets*, in which he imagined that intelligent beings overran our solar system. Earlier the mathematician and philosopher René Descartes had wondered whether "elsewhere there exist innumerable other creatures of higher quality than ourselves?" Scientists supplemented what they could glimpse through their telescopes with theological suppositions, like Johann Bode (1747–1826), the head of Berlin's observatory, who inquired whether the "most wise author of the world who assigns an insect lodging on a grain of sand" would fashion the endless expanse of space only to leave it empty of "rational inhabitants who are ready gratefully to praise the author of life?" An enlightened deity would presumably fill the galaxy with a multitude of reasonable beings, terrestrial and otherwise, and Paine agreed that "no part of space lies at waste, anymore than any part of the globe of earth and water is left unoccupied."

But Martians, "solarians," moon men and other aliens, some with minds and civilizations superior to our own, could hardly be expected to subscribe to Genesis, a book that lauds *Homo sapiens* as the culmination of Creation. "What are we to think of the Christian system of faith," Paine wondered, "that forms itself upon the idea of only one world?" The notion that the Almighty, "who had millions of worlds equally dependent on his protection, should quit the care of all the rest, and come to die in our world, because, they say, one man and one woman had eaten an apple" appeared a "solitary and strange conceit."

Within the plurality of worlds, how many "wild and whimsical systems of faith" had arisen, some praiseworthy and others pernicious but only one consistent with the facts of nature? As Paine pointed out, the Persians claimed their Zend-Avesta, the Muslims their Qur'an, the Jews their Torah, and the Brahmins their holy books, each calling their own scriptures "*revealed religion*, and the *only* true Word of God." Against such special pleading, natural religion looked directly to the universe for inspiration, the one revelation that all humanity, indeed all living beings everywhere, shared in common.

Although many labeled him an infidel for his biting dismissal of Christianity—Paine challenged the authenticity of miracles, including the resurrection, and he called the dogma of Mary's immaculate conception an old maid's tale—he was clearly more than an unbeliever. Actually, he sought to place belief in God upon a firmer footing, and he described his own creed in terms reminiscent of the prophet Micah:

> I believe in one God and no more, and I hope for happiness beyond this life. I believe in the equality of man; and I believe that religious duties consist in doing justice, loving mercy, and endeavouring to make our fellow creatures happy.

He called Jesus a "virtuous and amiable man" and agreed that the Bible contains "some good moral precepts" that should be respected and obeyed. For if Paine was opposed to religious expressions that he considered superstitious, he just as adamantly rejected godlessness. By forcibly dismantling the church, Paine feared, the French were in danger of absolutizing the state and deifying their revolutionary tribunals. Atheism in the new regime threatened to become a dogma, its proponents every bit as bloodthirsty as the inquisitors of old.

Were these the opinions of an infidel? "Infidelity does not consist in believing, or in disbelieving" in any case, Paine insisted. It consists in a person "professing to believe what he does not believe." Hypocrisy was the unforgivable sin in Paine's book, and by his own lights, he was a man of deep conviction.

In *The Age of Reason*, Paine called himself a Deist. But he also started his own religion, Theophilanthropy, which from its Greek roots means love to God and man. It was an ethical society, disavowing denominational affiliation. "The Theopilanthropists do not call themselves the disciples of such or such a man. They avail themselves of the wise precepts that have been transmitted by writers of all countries and in all ages." A book of readings for devotional use culled inspirational words from Greek and Asian poets, including Confucius, who had advocated a way of life based on virtue and right relation to one's community, with a minimum of theological baggage. Paine wasn't the only American who admired the Chinese sage. James Madison had a portrait of Confucius hanging in his dining room. Harmony and balance, reverence for education, and the ideal of the gentleman or "superior man" who leads by wisdom and example were all Confucian precepts that resonated with thinkers of the Enlightenment.

Yet Thomas Paine was no Confucianist. He was never a sectary, not even of a sect he founded himself. He was too iconoclastic to be bound by any official set of teachings. "I do not believe in the creed professed by the Jewish Church, by the Roman Church, by the Greek Church, by the Protestant Church, nor by any church that I know of," he bristled. "My own mind is my own church."

Thomas Paine was finally freed from French prison on November 4, 1794, through the intercessions of James Monroe, America's foreign minister to France, but only after more than ten months of "suffering exceedingly" and feeling betrayed by the first president, whose administration refused to even acknowledge him as a citizen. *The Crisis* had been composed at General Washington's entreaty, while *The Rights of Man* was dedicated to the commander in chief, who tried to help the author financially. The two men had often corresponded. So Paine's bitterness at being abandoned was compounded by what he imagined to be a personal affront. It is possible that Washington himself never learned of Paine's plight and was not quite as treacherous as his old friend imagined. But partisan politics were becoming increasingly acrimonious in the United States, and Paine blamed the Federalists, who he felt were subverting the original aims of the republic. Too ill to travel, he finally returned to the United States shortly after Jefferson's election as president in 1800. Although the chief executive welcomed the voyager home, even offering passage on a military warship, many tried to use their association to embarrass the new president.

Jefferson harbored many of the same beliefs and doubts as the returning exile. Once he likened the virgin birth to "the fable of the generation of Minerva in the brain of Jupiter." But the Virginian shared these sentiments in private, while the pugilistic Paine took the opposite tack. Exchanges with his enemies became toxic; it was an age of ad hominem attack. Even George Washington was called a "most horrid swearer and blasphemer" in the New York press. But no one was reviled like Thomas Paine, who was assaulted and threatened physically as well as verbally as an "obscene old sinner" and "the living opprobrium of humanity." The remaining years of his life were not happy ones.

But nothing can detract from Thomas Paine's legacy as an advocate of freedom. In the England where he was born, only one man in twenty could vote; in the whole of Scotland, fewer than three thousand people enjoyed the franchise. In the Constitution that Paine helped to write for his adopted state of Pennsylvania, the most progressive in the new nation, universal manhood suffrage was the rule. He championed the rights of the many against the privileges of the few.

He was the premier spokesman for American independence, and from the time of his arrival in America he wrote and agitated against slavery. As a member of the American Philosophical Society, he stood for an experimental approach to life that valued scientific method and a problem-solving temper. Paine was the quintessential immigrant—one who came to America in search of wider horizons and who helped open broader vistas for others.

And when it came to religious questions, he defended people's ability to think for themselves, never forsaking his Quaker assurance that every woman and man possessed a divine origin and an inner light that would lead them to discover God's presence within themselves and in the wider world. In *The Rights of Man*, he affirmed his faith "that what I am now doing, with an endeavor to conciliate mankind, to render their condition happy, to unite nations that have hitherto been enemies, and to extirpate the horrid practice of war, and break the chains of slavery and oppression, is acceptable in His sight, and being the best service I can perform, I act it cheerfully."

Though rumors of deathbed conversions abounded, he clung to his simple credo:

> The world is my country,
> All mankind are my brethren,
> To do good is my religion,
> I believe in one God and no more.

Thomas Paine never signed the Declaration of Independence. His only elective office was in France. But he belongs in the pantheon of America's founders nonetheless. For as John Adams remarked, the real insurrection in this country occurred long before the first shot was fired. "The Revolution was effected before the war commenced," Adams wrote. "The Revolution was in the minds and hearts of the people." It started when the settlers in the New World began to think of themselves as Americans rather than as English colonists. It gained a foothold when they learned to conceive of themselves as citizens rather than subjects. It won its chief victories in the collective consciousness, rather than by martial combat. Before the end of their lives, Adams and Paine would quarrel bitterly, but on this they could agree. "Our style and manner of thinking have undergone a revolution more extraordinary than the political revolution of the country," said *Common Sense*. "We see with other eyes; we hear with other ears; and think with other thoughts." No one did more to catalyze that change than Thomas Paine. He was, in his own words, a farmer of ideas who gave his crops away.

7.

Delight, Joy, Triumph, Exaltation

The Faith of John Adams

John Adams was a New Englander by ancestry and a Yankee by conviction. He was no cosmopolitan and could at times be self-conscious of his provincial roots and rather rustic manners. He was out of place amid the polished diplomats of Europe. His friend Jonathan Sewall observed that "He can't dance, drink, game, flatter, promise, dress, swear with the gentlemen, and small talk and flirt with the ladies—in short, he has none of the essential *arts* or *ornaments* which make a courtier."

Unlike Benjamin Franklin, whose raccoon cap became a badge of backwoods fashion, Adams suffered from being a country cousin. Yet at the same time, he was immensely proud of his hardscrabble pedigree. Refinements were superfluous to character, even if that character, like Adams's own, happened to be somewhat curmudgeonly and cantankerous. A self-described "grumbletonian," he made plainspoken and plain-dealing ways his trademark.

Appointed as American minister to the Court of St. James's after the war for independence, he delighted in confounding one of the foreign ministers who welcomed him to London. It was a tense interview, for Adams had been a ringleader in the rebellion of the thirteen colonies against the Crown. When others urged moderation, John and his cousin Samuel had agitated for more revolutionary action. Adams had been the primary spokesman for a Declaration of Independence in the Continental Congress, the one who nominated General George Washington to command the Continental armies; as chair of the Board of War and Ordnance his role in the Revolution had been roughly comparable to that of a modern-day secretary of defense. He'd even had the temerity to launch a United States Navy, testing England's supremacy on the seas. Now the former enemies had to find a way to be cordial to each other. His interlocutor attempted small talk first, inquiring into Adams's family history. "You have been often in England?" the minister asked. The American responded in the negative.

"You have relations in England, no doubt?"

"None at all."

"How can that be? You are of English extraction?"

"Neither my father or mother, grandfather or grandmother, great-grandfather or great-grandmother, nor any other relation that I know of, or care a farthing for, has been in England these one hundred and fifty years, so that you see I have not one drop of blood in my veins but what is American," Adams asserted proudly.

"Ay, we have seen proof enough of that," his interviewer conceded.

The fields might be stony on the northern coasts, but Adams was partial to his native land. Thrift, simple living, and a lack of ostentation were the bedrock of small-town life in Massachusetts and were almost synonymous with virtue in Adams's mind. The home in Braintree where he grew up was modest and functional, a two-story clapboard farmhouse with a central chimney and fireplace to provide heat for the four rooms where the family resided. John and his two brothers slept in cubbies under the eaves. It was an unremarkable structure, nearly indistinguishable from most other dwellings in town. Virtually any man with moderate energy might obtain a small freehold in Massachusetts, Adams noted with approval, and because the laws restricting the franchise to property holders were laxly enforced, practically any man could vote. A homespun equality prevailed, socially and economically.

In theory, Adams believed that a natural hierarchy existed among humankind. Some people would always be a bit more clever than others or possess abilities that distinguished them from the herd, and governments that failed to acknowledge this fact were in trouble. In his writings on the Constitution, he argued for a strong chief executive, as well as an upper house in the legislature to balance the power of the popular majority; to his later regret, he even used the word "monarch" to describe the executive role. During his term as president of the United States, he was accused of harboring imperial ambitions, and for suggesting that Washington ought to have a title capable of inspiring suitable awe for the office (Adams suggested "His Highness, president of the United States and Protector of the Liberties of the Same"), the portly patriot was jeered as "His Rotundity" by his enemies in Congress. Jefferson called the proposed title "the most superlatively ridiculous thing I ever heard of," recalling Ben Franklin's assessment of Adams as "always an honest man and often a just one, but sometimes absolutely mad." James Madison tactfully suggested the honorific "Mister President" would do just fine.

Yet in practice, Adams was an instinctive egalitarian. During the war for independence, he fought for greater parity of pay between officers and enlisted men, against southern delegates to the Continental Congress who were "accustomed, habituated, to higher notions of themselves and the distinction between them and the common people than we are." Adams found slavery repugnant. And after the war, he violently opposed the Order of the Cincinnati, because of its elitist character. Fearing that the Cincinnati—a hereditary guild of officers from the Revolution—would be the first step down the road to military dictatorship, he called it an illegal, dangerous organization and an "inroad upon our first principle, equality."

He was suspicious of finery, which bred decadence. "Luxury, wherever she goes, effaces from the human nature the image of the Divinity," predisposing people toward hedonism and a life of sensual pleasure rather than useful service. Were it in his power, he told his wife, Abigail (1744–1818), he would "forever banish and exclude from America all gold, silver, precious stones, alabaster, marble, silk, velvet and lace," even if the ladies denounced him as a "tyrant." Real tyrants, he reminded her, banished things of greater worth—virtue, wisdom, and liberty. Heading up a three-person commission to negotiate commercial treaties with France, he joined Jefferson and Franklin, the other members of the trio, outside Paris. His compatriots fit right into high society, but John and Abigail found their house at Auteuil too big for their taste. Though overlooking the Duc d'Orléans's castle at St. Cloud and a picturesque view of the river Seine, the French countryside could not compare to the familiar "hills of Penn and Neponsit, either in the grandeur or the beauty of the prospects." While enjoying the ballet and other cultural attractions, both just wanted to go home.

They yearned for the idylls of family life—"'Tis domestic happiness and rural felicity in the bosom of my native land that has charms for me," Abigail asserted—and their frequent separations produced a lifelong series of love letters as notable for their literary quality as their simmering passion. She managed the Braintree homestead in John's absence—a real feat since the little he received for his labors in Congress didn't even cover the expense of a hired man to help in the fields. Single parenting was no easier then than now, but Abigail also superintended the children's education, following her husband's exhortations as best she could: "Train them to virtue. Habituate them to industry, activity and spirit. Make them consider vice as shameful and unmanly. Fire them with ambition to be useful." Doubtless John hoped to replicate the kind of upbringing he experienced as a child.

As a boy, he'd wanted nothing more than to be a farmer. His father, seeking to instill some higher aspirations into his offspring, had taken the youngster with him into the marsh, to spend a wet, muddy, backbreaking day cutting and tying up bundles of thatching. That night the senior Adams challenged his son—"Well, John, are you satisfied with being a farmer?" "Yes, sir, I like it very well!" the lad replied. His father had other plans for him, but John's stubborn capacity for hard work would take him far in the world.

His forbears had settled in Braintree, a small farming village a few miles south of Boston, just ten years after the Puritans established their "city on a hill." The Massachusetts Bay Colony was intended to be a godly commonwealth that would provide the rest of the world with a vision of purified Christianity practiced according to the teachings of the Geneva reformer John Calvin. Adams was baptized into the faith in 1735 in a plain, boxlike meetinghouse that dominated the architecture of the town as much as the stern tenets of the religion dominated the minds of its inhabitants. In the little schoolhouse where Dame Belcher presided, the boy learned his alphabet, beginning with the letter A: "In Adam's fall, We sinned all." Together, the pupils recited their lessons:

> There is a dreadful fiery hell
> Where wicked ones must always dwell;
> There is a heaven full of joy,
> Where goodly ones must always stay;
> To one of these my soul must fly,
> As in a moment, when I die.

Sabbath observance was mandatory, and Adams remembered services in the church he attended as a boy when the sacramental bread was frozen hard as rock. The preaching could be equally indigestible, and as a young man he complained bitterly of the doctrines of the "frigid John Calvin."

Though he abandoned many other articles of faith, the doctrine of original sin continued to color Adams's view of the world throughout his life. He knew that people could be vain, ambitious, and frequently shortsighted—human beings were a fallen race—and he sometimes wrote in terms that recalled his religious upbringing. "To expect self-denial from men, when they have a majority in their favor, and consequently power to gratify themselves, is to disbelieve all history and universal experience," Adams declared many years later. "My fundamental maxim of government is, never to trust the lamb to the custody of the wolf." Checks and balances were the necessary restraints to keep arrogance and the lust for power within limits—to protect the minority from the majority and the individual from the mob.

He felt that crowds of people could be dangerous—like the throng that began pelting British sentries with rocks and snowballs in 1770, leading to the Boston Massacre. Adams defended the soldiers in court and managed to convince a jury that the Redcoats had fired in self-defense. Although he was no friend of the occupying armies, he was equally opposed to street gangs and vigilantism. Religious revivals worried him for the same reason. They deliberately inflamed emotions that ran counter to reason and good order. "Awakenings and Revivals are not peculiar to Religion," he warned. "Philosophy and Policy at times are capable of taking the Infection."

Lessons concerning government began early on, for like other New England villages, Braintree governed itself through a direct democracy. The church was where the town meeting was held each March. Deacons became selectmen, tithing men morphed into moderators, and business turned from the sacred to the mundane tasks of repairing the roads, caring for the indigent, and adopting a school budget. Although the stakes were small, the conflicts could be heated. Personalities collided, and tempers often flared. Shortly before Adams was born, a rule had to be passed forbidding citizens from standing up in their pews! Running for the town select board was Adams's first campaign for elective office. And the crankiness of his contentious neighbors probably shaped Adams's later attitudes toward the experiment of national self-government.

Church politics were perhaps the worst of all, and his departure from his childhood faith occurred when John was just ten. The church that year called a new minister, Lemuel Briant, and within a short time controversy "broke out like the Eruption of a Volcano and blazed with portentous aspect for many years." Briant was insufficiently orthodox for many in the congregation. One sermon with the daunting title "The Absurdity and Blasphemy of Depreciating Moral Virtue" gave particular offense for challenging the Calvinist doctrines of predestination and election by grace. John's father, a deacon, was somewhat sympathetic toward the beleaguered parson, while his uncle Ebenezer joined those seeking the preacher's ouster. Briant survived the inquisition that was held in the Adams's living room and served the parish for another four years. But the whole affair demonstrated for young John "a spirit of dogmatism and bigotry in clergy and laity" that left him disillusioned. "I perceived very clearly, as I thought, that the study of theology, and the pursuit of it as a profession, would involve me in endless altercations, and make my life miserable, without any prospect of doing any good to my fellow men." His parents' hopes that he might one day enter the ministry were permanently curdled by the incident.

John was at Harvard at the height of the tempest; he had enrolled at age fifteen to prepare himself for his life's work—

whatever that might be. Law seemed the most likely choice, for his university studies only confirmed his distaste for a vocation in the church. Harvard College had been established in 1636 as a seminary to educate the clergy of Puritan New England, but by the time Adams went there, a spirit of free inquiry had begun to infiltrate the campus. Abigail would observe that "infidelity abounds" at the university when their son Charles made preparation to attend a generation later. Scholars had long since begun to drift toward Deism under college president Edward Holyoke, known for his "catholic temper," and Harvard's Dudleian Lectures, founded in 1755 and dedicated to "the proving, explaining, and proper use and improvement of the principles of Natural Religion," were a sign of the times.

Most Christian apologists argued that religious knowledge derived from two sources: those truths that could be discovered through the unassisted intellect, from the evidences of Creation, and those that depended on special revelation, or the scriptures. Because they believed people's rational faculties had been dimmed by the Fall, the Puritans held that "We do not test the Bible by nature, but nature by the Bible." But under the influence of the Enlightenment, many had begun to argue that reason should be the primary guide. John Locke's writings had started to circulate in American universities early in the eighteenth century. In his *Two Treatises on Government*, he had written that critical thinking should be "our only star and compass" in interpreting biblical passages. The scriptures might suggest truths impossible to conclusively verify, but while faith might occasionally reach beyond logic, it should never run counter to it. "That there is a God, and what that God is," Locke asserted in one journal entry, "nothing can discover to us, nor judge in us, but natural reason."

That was Adams's conclusion, too. He eventually came to the position that "the human understanding is a revelation from its Maker, which can never be disputed or doubted," asserting that "we can never be so certain of any prophecy, or the fulfillment of any prophecy, or of any miracle, or the design of any miracle, as we are from the revelation of nature, that is, Nature's God, that two and two are equal to four." Nor could three be equal to one, he added with anti-Trinitarian emphasis. When revelation ran counter to common sense, reason had to prevail.

Adams was fascinated by his course of study in the sciences at Harvard under John Winthrop, the Hollis professor of mathematics and natural philosophy, "an excellent and happy teacher." Winthrop's paper detailing observations on Halley's comet had been read to the Royal Society in London by his friend Benjamin Franklin. For leading an expedition to Newfoundland to observe the transit of Venus, Winthrop was later inducted as a Royal Society fellow himself. In addition to original research, his teaching duties were to instruct the students in "Pneumaticks, Hydrostaticks, Mechanicks, Statics, Opticks," algebra, geometry, and trigonometry, as well as "the principles of Astronomy and Geography, viz. . . . the use of globes, the motions of heavenly bodies according to the different hypotheses of Ptolemy, Tycho Brahe, and Copernicus." Harvard had the best scientific curriculum and instrumentation of any American university at that time. Gazing through Professor Winthrop's telescopes at the satellites of Jupiter was to prove a high point of Adams's education there.

The attraction was lifelong. His diaries from midlife were interspersed with scientific inquiries: "What is it in the air which burns? When we blow a spark with the bellows, it spreads. We force a current of air to the fire, by this machine, and in this air are inflammable particles. Can it be in the same manner that life is continued by the breath? Are there particles conveyed into the blood of animals through the lungs which increase the heat of it?" He speculated that respiration might "carry in some particles that are salubrious, and carry out others which are noxious." From these reflections he turned to a series of mental experiments involving magnetism. Noting that "the lodestone is in possession of the most remarkable, wonderful and mysterious property in nature," a power of attraction and repulsion invisible to the microscope yet operating throughout the earth from pole to pole, he wondered in his journal, "Has it been tried, whether the magnet loses any of its force in a vacuo? In a bottle charged with electrical fire, etc.?" He proposed grinding magnets to powder, steeping them in chemicals, burning and freezing them to see if their efficacy were affected. Adams had little opportunity to carry out such scientific investigations himself. But as American emissary to England, he did have an opportunity to visit with William Herschel (1738–1822), who discovered the planet Uranus and was the first to correctly describe the shape of the Milky Way galaxy, at Britain's Royal Observatory. Unfortunately, the night was overcast, so there was no stargazing. But John found him a "cheerful and intelligent companion; communicative of his knowledge and very agreeable" to showing his visitor his apparatus and bringing him up-to-date on the latest discoveries. Daughter Nabby wrote in her journal, "I have never known him to be so much gratified by a visit of any kind before."

Scientific learning opened new vistas on the heavens for Adams and raised theological questions as well. "Astronomers tell us with good reason, that not only all the planets and

satellites in our solar system, but all the unnumbered worlds
that revolve around the fixed stars are inhabited, as well as
this globe of earth," he mused. Herschel himself had seen evidence of roads, canals, and other structures on the moon and
was convinced the sun was likewise "a most magnificent hab-
itable globe." With so many sentient beings and civilizations
scattered across the cosmos, Adams asked, did it make sense
to believe that "God Almighty must assume the respective
shapes of all these different species" in the form of a savior, or
that "all these beings must be consigned to everlasting perdi-
tion?" The supposition was hard to swallow.

Traditional notions of salvation were crumbling. As Adams
considered the intricacy of the universe, he reflected, "The
minutest particle, in one of Saturn's satellites, may have some
influence upon the most distant regions of the system." His
conception of the cosmos as an energetic field of interacting
forces sounds almost modern:

> Our system, considered as one body hanging on its center of
> gravity, may affect and be affected by all the other systems
> within the compass of creation. Thus it is highly probable
> every particle of matter influences and is influenced by ev-
> ery other particle in the whole collected universe.

Could the God who created this immensity have possibly been
incarnated in the form of a Galilean peasant nearly two thousand years ago? It was impossible for Adams to believe that
this "great principle, which has produced this boundless Universe, Newton's Universe, and Hershells universe, came down
to this little Ball," to be executed like a sordid criminal.

Nor would a deity of such cosmic proportions indulge in

petty human emotions of petulance or retribution. Could a Creator whose "presence is as extensive as space" have made the human race, only to consign nine-tenths of them to eternal fire? "Now, my friend, can prophecies or miracles convince you or me that infinite benevolence, wisdom and power, created, and preserved for a time, innumerable millions, to make them miserable forever, for his own glory? What is his glory? Is he ambitious? Does he want promotion? Is he vain, tickled with adulation, exulting and triumphing in his power and the sweetness of his vengeance?" Adams did believe in a state of future rewards and punishments, but the doctrine of everlasting damnation was a libel upon the character of an otherwise compassionate Creator. As he wrote to Thomas Jefferson, "I believe no such things":

> My adoration of the Author of the Universe is too profound and too sincere. The love of God and his creation—delight, joy, triumph, exaltation in my own existence—though but an atom, a molecule *organique* in the universe—are my religion.

Small wonder that Adams and Jefferson alike were accused of infidelity. The *Christian Watchman* in 1823 chided the "heathenish" tendency of both presidents to speak of the divine in naturalistic rather than strictly biblical terms, as "the Great Teacher" or "Ruler of the Skies."

Yet Adams maintained that he was a true Christian, against all who questioned the bona fides of his faith. "The Christian religion is, above all the religions that ever prevailed or existed in ancient or modern times, the religion of wisdom, virtue, equity, and humanity," he insisted; "it is resignation to God, it is goodness itself to man." He admitted that other religions might also contain a saving truth, and looked forward to "translations into English and French, Spanish and German and Italian of sacred books of Persians, the Chinese, the Hindoos, etc., etc., etc. Then our grandchildren and my great-grandchildren may compare notes and hold fast all that is good." But he had little doubt that Christianity would commend itself to people of every land, supplemented but never supplanted by the precepts of other traditions. "The Christian religion, as I understand it, is the brightness of the glory and the express portrait of the character of the eternal, self-existent, independent, benevolent, all powerful and all merciful creator, preserver, and father of the universe, the first good, first perfect, and first fair."

The key phrase in this testament is Adams's proviso, "as I understand it." Christianity for him centered in the ethical teachings of Jesus and the Hebrew prophets. "The Ten Commandments and the Sermon on the Mount contain my religion," he proclaimed. Unfortunately, the church had wandered far from the simple parables of its founder. Organized religion often seemed more concerned with institutional self-maintenance than with improving morals or transforming lives. "Where do we find a precept in the Gospel requiring Ecclesiastical Synods? Convocations? Councils? Decrees? Creeds? Confessions? Oaths? Subscriptions? and whole cartloads of other trumpery that we find religion encumbered with in these days?" Adams asked. "How has it happened that millions of fables, tales, legends, have been blended with both Jewish and Christian revelation that have made them the most bloody religion that ever existed?" Most churches seemed to have lost their reason for being. "The design of Christianity was not to make men good riddle-solvers or good mystery-mongers," he complained, "but good men, good magistrates, and good subjects, good husbands and good wives, good parents and good children, good masters and good servants." Clearly Adams felt that many Christian sects had failed in this task—including the Puritanical lineage of his youth.

Later in life, he mellowed somewhat toward his childhood faith. "I must be a very unnatural son to entertain any prejudices against the Calvinists," he told the Reverend Samuel Miller in 1820, "for my father and mother, my uncles and aunts, and all my predecessors, from our common ancestor, who landed in this country two hundred years ago were of that persuasion. Indeed, I have never known any better people than the Calvinists." From his spiritual forbears, John Adams inherited a high moral seriousness and strict code of personal conduct that served him well throughout his life, along with the work ethic for which Puritans were famous. He also inherited a rather gloomy disposition—he was prone to periods of despondency—and a view of the human situation that looked upon life as nothing more than "a vapor, a fog, a dew, a cloud, a blossom." But like the Puritans, who knew that "the flower fadeth," he could still sing praises to the Creator of it all. "I cannot class myself under that denomination," Adams concluded his letter to Miller, but he could still be grateful for the soil from which he sprang.

Attending weekly worship was one part of the Puritan legacy that never left him. "It is notorious enough that I have been a church-going animal for seventy-six years, from the cradle," he told Benjamin Rush. Like Washington, who believed that churchgoing was a tonic for the health of the republic, Adams recommended "regular attendance on public worship as a means of moral instruction and social improvement."

Unlike Washington, Adams seldom missed a Sunday. One year an epidemic of dysentery ran through Braintree that gripped so many of the residents the local parish had to be closed for four successive weeks. Abigail could hardly move, and Pastor Wibird was as sick as the others. Canceling church was an unheard-of event almost as upsetting as the illness itself.

When traveling, Adams visited other congregations. He was curious enough to visit a "Romish chapel" on at least one occasion, where he found the music "exquisitely soft and sweet." Even though he disapproved of the priests "chanting Latin, not a word of which they understood," the ritual was more powerful than he expected. "I am amazed that Luther and Calvin were ever able to break the charm and dissolve the spell," he confided to a friend.

In New York, where he was stationed during his tenure as George Washington's immediate subordinate (he bitterly described the vice presidency as "the most insignificant office that was the invention of man"), he and Abigail struggled to find a church to their liking. The Congregational preachers there clung to the old-fashioned doctrines of predestination and tried with "noise and vehemence to compensate for every other deficiency." Listening to their "foaming," Abigail told a friend, was like "doing penance," making her long to hear "liberal good sense" from the pulpit: "true piety without enthusiasm, devotion without grimace, and religion upon a rational system."

More to their tastes were the sermons of Richard Price (1723–91), a dissenting clergyman whose services the two attended while on appointment to Great Britain. Although ordained a Presbyterian, Price's doubts about the divinity of Jesus had turned him toward Unitarianism—like his friend Joseph

Priestley, who succeeded him in the same pulpit. A superb mathematician, Price shared Adams's scientific interests. When the reverend presided over the christening of their grandchild William, Abigail was so flustered that she had to take to her bed, causing her to miss several of his lectures on "electricity, magnetism, hydostatics" and other researches which she described as "going into a beautiful country . . . a country to which few females are permitted to visit or inspect."

Dr. Price had been a strong supporter of the colonies in their revolt against England. In *Observations on the Importance of the American Revolution, and the Means of Making It a Benefit to the World*, published just after the war for independence, Price argued that complete religious liberty ought to prevail in the new nation, along with a system of education that "teaches *how* to think, rather than *what* to think." He spoke admiringly of the Massachusetts Constitution that Adams had written, guaranteeing that "every denomination of Christians demeaning themselves peaceably and as good subjects of the commonwealth" should have equal protection of the law. "This is liberal beyond all example," Price declared. "I should, however, have admired it more had it been more liberal, and the words, *all men of all religions* been substituted for the words *every denomination of Christians.*"

Massachusetts maintained a religious establishment, but no one creed was officially sanctioned by the government, and no sect superior or subordinate to another. Within limits, citizens could direct their taxes to whatever church they happened to attend. "I am happy to find myself perfectly agreed with you, that we should begin by setting conscience free," Adams wrote to Dr. Price. It was the foundation of a lifelong friendship, and Abigail wrote their son John Quincy that traveling the distance from London to Hackney was well worth the effort each Sunday "to hear a man so liberal and so sensible and so good as he is."

That distance was not nearly as far as Adams would eventually travel on his spiritual journey—one that would take him far from the Calvinism of his youth. At the age of eighty, he would summarize his beliefs as follows:

> My religion is founded on the love of God and my neighbor; on the hope of pardon for my offences; upon contrition; upon the duty as well as the necessity of supporting with patience the inevitable evils of life; in the duty of doing no wrong, but all the good I can, to the creation, of which I am but an infinitesimal part.

He had come a long way from the stern lessons of Miss Belcher's schoolhouse.

An open mind and insatiable curiosity had propelled his thinking along the way. "Before I was twenty years old," he told John Quincy, "I resolved never to be afraid to read any book," and he never repented of the resolution, for the written word fed his appreciation for the greatest Author of all. "I want to study the Chaldean language," he remarked toward the end of life. "I want to read all the Christian Fathers and the Ecclesiastical historians. I want to learn the Chinese language, and to study all the Asiatic researches," hoping for another thousand years to plow through the unread titles on his book list.

Yet however far Adams ventured, spiritually or physically, he always came back to Braintree and to the meetinghouse where his family had worshiped for generations—and where he would eventually be laid to rest. Walking the farm that he

named Peacefield, riding horseback in the countryside, surveying the familiar Blue Hills of his childhood, and playing with
his own grandchildren brought comfort to his later years.

His presidency had been wracked by dissension. Rejected at
the polls after a single term in office, he lamented that "if I were
to go over my life again, I would be a shoemaker rather than an
American statesman." But there was something healing in the
changing seasons and never-ending round of chores that constituted rural life. As a boy, he had wanted only to muck about the
fields. Finally, his wish was fulfilled. He had "exchanged honor
and virtue for manure," he joked to a friend. But the landscape
reminded him of life's continuities—and so did the persistence
of faith. "What has preserved this race of Adamses in all their
ramifications, in such numbers, health, peace, comfort and
mediocrity?" he asked rhetorically. Except for the bulwark of
religion, they might have all been "rakes, fops, sots, gamblers,
starved with hunger, frozen with cold, scalped by Indians, etc.,
etc., etc., been melted away and disappeared."

Adams paid tribute to that heritage in the words he inscribed
on the lid of the sarcophagus of his great-great-grandfather
Henry—the first of the Adams line to emigrate from England
and settle in Massachusetts Bay in 1640:

> This stone and several others have been placed in this yard
> by a great, great, grandson from a veneration of the piety,
> humility, simplicity, prudence, frugality, industry and per-
> severance of his ancestors in hopes of recommending an af-
> firmation of their virtues to their posterity.

In retrospect, he had many reasons to be grateful. Though
fate had handed him "a pretty large dose" of distress and pain,

still he had enjoyed "more pleasure than pain ten to one, nay, if you please, an hundred to one." In Abigail, he'd found his lifelong soul mate and intellectual companion. A son had followed in his footsteps to the highest office in the land. He was conscious that he had lived in historic times and had a hand in shaping events with worldwide repercussions.

As his thoughts turned toward futurity, he wrote, "I am not tormented with the fear of death; nor though suffering under many infirmities and agitated by many afflictions, weary of life . . . we shall leave the world with many consolations; it is better than we found it—superstition, persecution, and bigotry are somewhat abated, governments are a little ameliorated, science and literature are greatly improved and more widely spread. Our country has brilliant and exhilarating prospects before it."

Yet he composed no epitaph for himself, no lengthy litany of his own attainments. Chalk it up to Yankee reserve, or to the genuine modesty that was the flip side of his own enormous ego, but at the end of his life, he left behind only a few words of homage to the past and a wish that the future might live up to the promise of those sturdy New England pioneers from whom he traced his own descent. It was the perfect monument, carved from native rock—as solid, durable, and understated as the man who put it there.

8.

Question with Boldness

---•·••·•---

The Faith of Thomas Jefferson

Thomas Jefferson was just as smooth as John Adams was angular. Even dressed down in house slippers and old clothes—a "republican" affectation he adopted during his first term as president to advertise his common touch—the Virginian was as suave and charming as the New Englander was dour and blunt.

When the Chevalier de Chastellux, a member of the French Academy of Sciences, visited Jefferson at his home in Albemarle County in 1782, he described "a man, not yet forty, tall, and with a mild and pleasing countenance, but whose mind and understanding are ample substitutes for every exterior grace. An American, who without ever having quitted his own country, is at once a musician, skilled in drawing, a geometrician, an astronomer, a natural philosopher, legislator and statesman." The admiring guest might have added that his host was also an able architect, educator, cartographer, classicist, biblical scholar, and inventor—an ideal gentleman of the Enlightenment.

Surveying the Italian-inspired pavilion of Monticello, the chevalier did remark that "Mr. Jefferson is the first American who has consulted the fine arts to know how he should shelter himself from the weather." By that time, the hilltop abode had been under construction for fourteen years, affording its occupant an exquisite view of the surrounding country. The home was a work in progress like its owner—perpetually brimming with new ideas and discarding others, an edifice in continuous improvement.

Russet haired and ramrod straight with arms characteristically folded across his chest, the American seemed aloof at first, but then warmed as the two philosophers discovered their common interests, amusing themselves over a punch-bowl, quoting antique poetry as they watched the sun fading over the mountains. "From his youth," exclaimed the French visitor, "he had placed his mind, as he had done his house, on an elevated situation, from which he might contemplate the universe." Jefferson brought a glimmer of genius to every field he touched.

His interests were encyclopedic. As a linguist, he compiled extensive vocabularies of Native American languages and fairly introduced the study of anthropology to North America.

Anglo-Saxon history and Chinese temple design were equally within his ken. He surrounded himself with fossils, botanical specimens, and his own ingenious contraptions, like a revolving bookcase, the better to access his enormous library. He collected and perfected instruments: telescopes, timepieces, surveying tools, letterpresses, and the "polygraph"—a device for instantly copying handwritten letters to which he made so many improvements that it might fairly be called his own creation.

The eighteenth-century version of a duplicator, the polygraph enabled him to carry on a vast correspondence. In a bequest to his grandson, Jefferson estimated that he had written about forty thousand letters over the span of his lifetime—carefully copying and filing each one. By this means, he kept abreast of the latest technology, sharing brainstorms with Robert Fulton, Eli Whitney, and other savants about balloon aviation, a ship propelled by a screw, the possibility of submarine navigation, and the use of steam to turn grist mills—an energy source that held great potential for the nation's future, in his estimation.

If George Washington's portrait occupies the place of honor on the dollar bill, Jefferson deserves most of the credit for creating our currency. Anxious to rid Americans of the computational confusion of doing sums in pounds, schillings, and farthings, Jefferson recommended the establishment of a decimal system for coinage, a suggestion that Congress readily adopted. If he had his way, weights and measures would also have been rationalized. Tasked with finding a standard and universal unit of length, Jefferson tried to locate a "natural" index of measurement by looking to the earth's unvarying rotation, which could be reduced to hours and then seconds:

> Let the standard of measure, then, be a uniform, cylindrical
> rod of iron, of such length as, in latitude 45° in the level of
> the ocean, and in a cellar, or other place, the temperature of
> which does not vary through the year, shall perform its vibra-
> tions in small and equal arcs, in one second of mean time.

The technical reasons behind the recommendation are arcane,
but everyone knows that a system with 12 inches to a foot,
3 feet in a yard, and 1,760 yards to a mile gets cumbersome.
Jefferson tried to simplify all that. While he himself found the
study of mathematics "peculiarly engaging and delightful," he
realized that when it comes to fractions, "the bulk of mankind
are school-boys through life." Had his version of the metric
plan been adopted, it might have brought "the calculations of
the principal affairs of life within the arithmetic of every man
who can multiply and divide plain numbers."

After Franklin, he was the most accomplished naturalist
among the founders, and had circumstances permitted, he
might have dedicated full time to his avocation. "Nature intended me for the tranquil pursuits of science," he confided
to the economist Pierre-Samuel Dupont de Nemours, "by
rendering them my supreme delight." Though he spent a lifetime in politics—serving in Virginia's House of Burgesses, as
governor of his home state in war time, spending five years
as America's minister plenipotentiary to France, and holding
other assorted offices including secretary of state under George
Washington, head of the United States Patent Office, and two
terms as the nation's president—government service ranked
lower in his esteem than the life of the mind. "Nobody can
conceive that nature ever intended to throw away a Newton
upon the occupations of a crown," as he put it.

So when he traveled to Philadelphia to take his oath of office as vice president of the United States—having lost the election of 1796 to John Adams—Jefferson was less than enthusiastic about his new station. He was much more hopeful about his concurrent elevation to the presidency of the American Philosophical Society, headquartered in the same city, anticipating that playing second fiddle to his old friend and rival might afford him "philosophical evenings in the winter and rural days in the summer" to pursue his real passion. Jefferson's first official act, a week after his installation as vice president, was to lecture the society on a set of prehistoric remains discovered in a cave in Greenbrier County, Virginia, that he believed belonged to a *Megalonyx* or "Great Claw." Judging from the thighbone, forearm, and several nails in his possession, he estimated the beast was three times bigger than a lion—a regal animal that proved the New World, including his native state, could produce wildlife on a majestic scale.

European naturalists, particularly the Comte de Buffon, had suggested that plants and animals tended to grow puny on American soil, so for chauvinistic reasons the Virginian was delighted with the find. Thrilled, he and Benjamin Rush speculated that the *Megalonyx* was a fierce predator that had gone extinct when lesser creatures joined in combination to bring about its downfall—a paleontological parable of the thirteen colonies casting off a voracious despot. Unfortunately, the "Great Claw" turned out to be a giant ground sloth rather than anything like the king of beasts. But Jefferson accepted the correction with scientific detachment, subscribing to Buffon's dictum that "I love a man who corrects me in an error as much as one who apprehends me of a truth, for in effect an error corrected is a truth." His mental equanimity was exceeded only by his appetite for knowledge.

As a boy, Thomas received fairly conventional religious training. He learned his prayers from his mother and listened to his older sister sing psalms. The moral precepts he absorbed may have been similar to the counsel he offered in later years to another growing child: "Adore God. Reverence and cherish your parents. Love your neighbor as yourself and your country more than yourself. Be just. Be true. Murmur not at the ways of Providence." With another youngster he shared "A Decalogue of Canons."

1. Never put off until tomorrow what you can do to-day.
2. Never trouble another for what you can do yourself.
3. Never spend your money before you have it.
4. Never buy what you do not want, because it is cheap; it will be dear to you.
5. Pride costs us more than hunger, thirst and cold.
6. We never repent for having eaten too little.
7. Nothing is troublesome that we do willingly.
8. How much pain has cost us the evils which have never happened?
9. Take things always by their smooth handle.
10. When angry count ten, before you speak; if very angry, one hundred.

As a parent, he was strict but doting. Daughter Martha recalled her father admonishing her to heed the monitions of conscience and urging her to industry: "No person will have occasion to complain of the want of time who never loses any." In France, the girl would briefly attend a convent school, but was withdrawn when *père* saw her growing enchantment with the nuns.

His own earliest tutors were both clergymen and though he chafed under the instruction of the first (a Presbyterian), the second, the Reverend James Maury of the Fredricksville Anglican Parish in Virginia, imparted a love of classical literature along with a proficiency in Latin and Greek that lasted Jefferson a lifetime. But an affinity for nature must have been instilled from an early age, too. His appreciation of the outdoors bordered on the spiritual:

> How sublime to look down into the workhouse of nature, to see her clouds, hail, snow, rain thunder, all fabricated at our feet! And the glorious Sun, when rising as if out of a distant water, just gilding the tops of the mountains, and giving life to all nature!

Botany he ranked as the most useful branch of human learning, and among his chief inventions was a more efficient plow. To artist Charles Willson Peale he wrote that "I have often thought that if heaven had given me choice of my position and calling, it should have been on a rich spot of earth, well watered, and near a good market for the production of the garden. No occupation is so delightful to me as the culture of the earth." His vision of the good life was agrarian. "Those who labour in the earth are the chosen people of God," he professed, while "the mobs of great cities add just so much to the support of pure government, as sores do to the strength of the human body." No urbanite, he regarded Paris as an "empty bustle" and, while he adored the bookstalls along the Seine, he remained suspicious of city dwellers all his life.

Peter Jefferson, his father, had settled the family on a site overlooking the Rivanna River to the south with the Blue Ridge

Mountains visible in the distant west. It was still wild country, sparsely populated. Though his agricultural holdings were not especially large, his wife was a Randolph, giving him influential connections. Besides becoming a justice of the peace and member of the Burgesses, Peter taught himself the mathematics needed for mapmaking and was appointed county surveyor. Thomas was just fourteen in 1757 when his father died, leaving him an estate of several thousand acres, along with a small collection of books and surveyor's gear. Tradition holds that Peter's dying wish was for his son to receive a first-rate education.

The College of William and Mary provided a foundation that Jefferson said "fixed the destinies" of his later career. The man most responsible for his schooling was William Small, professor of natural philosophy, the only member of the seven-man faculty not ordained in the Church of England. One lesson he imparted to his famous pupil was the importance of maintaining intellectual independence. Small quit the college shortly after Jefferson graduated in a dispute over academic freedom; when the governing board insisted that faculty members could be dismissed at will, he resigned and returned to Birmingham, England, where he joined Priestley, Erasmus Darwin, and other freewheeling thinkers of the Lunar Society. Described by Jefferson as a man with "an enlarged and liberal mind," Small probably contributed to the school's reputation as a cradle of Deism. The Reverend William Robinson, the college president, reported in discouragement to the bishop of London that unless the institution were brought under stricter ecclesiastical control it would never do much to foster religion in the colony.

During his tenure in Williamsburg, Small introduced his pupil to the "expansion of science" that was widening human understanding, including the theories of Isaac Newton (1642–1727). Like the ancient geometer Euclid, who had based his theorems on a set of preexisting postulates, Newton in the *Principia* developed a set of mathematical axioms from which conclusions about the laws of motion could be rigorously derived. In his *Opticks*, Newton warned the student against the indulging in untested hypotheses and showed how to pose and answer questions directly at the workbench, lessons amplified in Desaguliers's *A Course in Experimental Philosophy*. Jefferson was entranced. "We have no theories there, no uncertainties remain on the mind; all is demonstration and satisfaction."

Reason became Jefferson's guiding star. He exhorted his nephew Peter Carr, "Question with boldness even the existence of God, because, if there is one, he must more approve the homage of reason, than that of blind-folded fear." For Jefferson, neither tradition nor holy books nor popular opinion held the same authority as his own discriminating intellect. "Reason and free inquiry are the only effectual agents against error," he insisted in his *Notes on the State of Virginia*. "Give a loose to them, they will support the true religion by bringing every false one to their tribunal."

Newton was his paragon, along with Francis Bacon (1561–1626) and John Locke, "the three greatest men that have ever lived." And like Locke, whose *Two Treatises on Government* were among the first volumes he purchased for his own personal library, Jefferson believed the power of reason could uncover moral truths, in addition to scientific ones. Famously, these truths included the proposition that all men are created equal. His original draft of the Declaration of Independence stated that "We hold these truths to be sacred and undeniable," but the phrase was altered in the final version (probably at Benjamin Franklin's urging) to suggest that certain human rights are "self-evident," more like the truths deduced from a syllogism or scientific demonstration than like those acquired through religious experience. And where Locke had stipulated that these rights include "life, liberty and property," Jefferson substituted for possessions the felicitous and more encompassing phrase "pursuit of happiness."

The Declaration received its first public proclamation atop an astronomical platform in Philadelphia erected in 1769 to observe the transit of Venus: a fitting location, for reason told Jefferson that freedom was a gift from above. As he had written in his *Summary View* two years before, "the God who gave us life gave us liberty at the same time." But the Creator invoked in the Declaration was "nature and nature's God." One historian has counted twenty-six different names that Jefferson used for this Supreme Being, including Intelligent and Powerful Agent, Deity, Common Father, Giver of Life, and Infinite Power. This Power was not entirely impersonal. Like Washington, who employed at least fifty-four designations for the divine, from Giver of Life to Superintending Providence, Jefferson believed in a "Providence which governs the destinies of men and nations." But the transcendent stood revealed primarily in the wonders of Creation. Contemplating "the movements of the heavenly bodies, so exactly held in their courses by the balance of centrifugal and centripetal forces," along with the earth and its plenitude of creatures, "it is impossible not to believe, that there is in all this, design, cause and effect, up to an ultimate cause, a Fabricator of all things from matter and motion."

His Fabricator was as civilized as himself—far more rational and enlightened than the divinities of old. Jefferson termed

John Calvin's capricious deity, predestining some souls to bliss and the vast majority to eternal flames, a "malignant daemon" rather than a being worthy of reverence. The doctrine of the Trinity he considered "an unintelligible proposition of Platonic mysticisms that three are one, and one is three; and yet one is not three, and the three are not one." In good conscience, he refused to act as godfather at the baptism of his friends' children because he could not honestly profess his belief in the Apostles' Creed that was part of the Anglican service. Ironically, he was spared this dilemma in the case of his own children, since the church at that time didn't require from parents the same confession of belief.

Jefferson remained an Episcopalian all his life and was buried by the Reverend Frederick Hatch, the teacher of his grandsons and pastor of a small church in Charlottesville that Jefferson had designed. As president, he accompanied his daughters to Sunday services in the halls of Congress. Yet his accounting records show support for a variety of denominations: "I have subscribed to the building of an Episcopal church, two hundred dollars; a Presbyterian, sixty dollars; and a Baptist twenty-five dollars." During his first term in the White House, he pressed the commissioners of the newly established District of Columbia to grant the request of a Catholic church to purchase land in the capitol district. He felt the republic gained from religious diversity. While differing in outward form, he said in his inaugural address, all faiths tended to inculcate "honesty, truth, temperance, gratitude" and other virtues. "I believe, with the Quaker preacher, that he who observes those moral precepts in which all religions concur, will never be questioned at the gates of heaven as to the dogmas in which they all differ." Creeds might divide humankind, but on the fundamentals of morality most religions converged. And the very multiplicity of sects guarded against the dominance of any one that might otherwise tend toward spiritual tyranny.

While avoiding identification with any one denomination, he tended toward Unitarianism theologically, and like John Adams worshiped more than once in the chapel that his fellow scientist the Reverend Joseph Priestley had founded in Northumberland, outside Philadelphia. The two did not meet until 1797, when Jefferson was installed as vice president— Priestley was at the *Megalonyx* lecture the following week. But the Virginian claimed to have read Priestley's two volumes on *The Corruptions of Christianity* "over and over." It was Priestley who encouraged him to clarify his thoughts about Jesus.

In the spring of 1803, the Englishman sent his friend a pamphlet he had written titled *Socrates and Jesus Compared*. The recipient had already dedicated considerable attention to the subject. In his youth, Jefferson studied the philosophers of classical antiquity. And just as the Greek and Roman style shaped his architectural preferences in designing Monticello, the rationality and balance of Socrates, Seneca, Cicero, and Epicurus appealed to his desire for a life disciplined by inward harmony and self-control.

For gentlemen of the Enlightenment, classical learning offered an alternative (and in some cases an anteroom) to Christian faith. Thinkers like Seneca provided men like Washington and Jefferson with models of dignified comportment: how to live with equanimity and die without fear. "The Roman Stoic," according to historian Will Durant, "was a man of action rather than contemplation," eschewing metaphysics in favor of cultivating courage, candor, and other worldly virtues, "conduct that would support human decency, family unity, and social order independently of supernatural surveillance and command." For those ready to pledge their lives, fortunes, and sacred honor on America's behalf, the traits that defined the Stoic had irresistible appeal:

> In politics he would recognize the universal brotherhood of man under the fatherhood of God; at the same time he would love his country and hold himself ready to die at any time to avert its disgrace or his own. Life itself was always to remain within his choice; he was free to leave it whenever it should become an evil rather than a boon. A man's conscience was to be higher than any law.

While not exactly Jeffersonian democrats—monarchy might be a sad necessity for the governance of wide and diverse realms—the Stoics nonetheless recognized that "to kill a despot was an excellent thing."

In addition to all this, Seneca wrote the *Quaestiones Naturales*, seeking scientific explanations for earthquakes and volcanoes, lightning and thunder, rainbows and rivers. "Before you judge, investigate!" he warned. Noticing that miners tunneling in the earth had never stumbled across anything resembling Tartarus (the Roman equivalent of hell), he questioned the reality of an underworld. "Those things which make the infernal regions terrible, the darkness, the prison, the river of flaming fire, the judgment seat, &c., are all a fable, with which the poets amuse themselves, and by them agitate us with vain terrors." Born in 4 BC, contemporaneous with Christ, he and other Stoics offered a philosophy of life at times complementing, but frequently conflicting with, the teachings of the church.

Early on, Jefferson called himself an Epicurean, a lifestyle he described as devoted to "ease of body and tranquility of mind." All his years, he enjoyed good food, fine wine (but not hard spirits), beautiful art, and finely made belongings. In Williamsburg, where he practiced law, Jefferson rarely missed an opportunity to attend the theater. He liked to dance and play the violin. But life's pleasures should be savored in moderation, he believed. Happiness might be the goal of life, but knowledge and virtue were the foundation of contentment.

As a young man, Jefferson felt the pagan philosophers offered a "more full, more entire, more coherent" ethic than the Bible. By the time Priestley sent his pamphlet, however, Jefferson had reassessed. Epicurus and the Stoics seemed too concerned with self-fulfillment. "Their precepts related chiefly to ourselves" and were less occupied with duty and service to others. Unable to convince Priestley to expand his pamphlet, Jefferson put his own thoughts on paper to amplify his growing sense of the superiority of Christian morals.

He began with an overview of New Testament times. Jefferson characterized the Jews of the first century as a people gone spiritually astray—obsessed with empty ceremonialism, proud and clannish in their claim to be a chosen people, worshiping a petty and vengeful deity. This was surely an unfair portrait, and he was no anti-Semite. He told the rabbi of the synagogue in Savannah, Georgia, that the religious freedom guaranteed by the United States Constitution would "restore to the Jews their social rights," while admitting to another Jewish correspondent that much still needed to be done to eliminate the "prejudices still scowling on your religion." While Jefferson was fluent in Greek, he had no acquaintance with Hebrew, so his knowledge of the Hebrew Bible and the Jewish context of early Christianity was limited. His depiction of Judaism missed the mark—the man from Nazareth was as much an outgrowth of his Jewish milieu as an exception to it. But Jefferson was right that Jesus was more concerned with compassion than with ritual purity and that he challenged the religious establishment of his day:

> In this state of things among the Jews, Jesus appeared. His parentage was obscure; his condition poor; his education null; his natural endowments great; his life correct and innocent: he was meek, benevolent, patient, firm, disinterested, & of the sublimest eloquence.

In Jefferson's view, the beauty of Jesus's words and deeds were nearly lost, his teachings scattered among peasants who committed their memories to writing only long after he was gone. Most of what his followers remembered became garbled, "mutilated, misstated, and often unintelligible," infused with the "mysticisms" of neo-Platonists. Paul was the main culprit in subverting the master's teachings, along with Athanasius, who overlaid the "metaphysical insanity" of the Trinity atop the historical Jesus. "According to the ordinary fate of those who attempt to enlighten and reform mankind, he fell an early victim to the jealousy of the altar and the throne, entrenched with power and riches." Yet neither the pomp of the church nor the power of the state had been able to completely obscure the Galilean's message. "Notwithstanding these disadvantages, a system of morals is presented to us, which, if filled up in the true style and spirit of the rich fragments he left us, would be the most perfect and sublime that has ever been taught by man." If not a messiah or divine savior, Jesus was still the greatest spiritual reformer of all time.

These thoughts, summarized in a "Syllabus of an Estimate of the Merit of the Doctrines of Jesus, Compared with those of Others," were "the result of a life of inquiry and reflection," Jefferson said in a letter to Dr. Benjamin Rush that accompanied the document. He also sent copies to Priestley and a few other confidants, stipulating that the contents remain under seal. He was anxious to dispel rumors that he was somehow anti-Christian. As he explained to Rush, "To the corruptions of Christianity I am indeed opposed, but not to the genuine precepts of Jesus himself. I am a Christian, in the only sense he wished any one to be; sincerely attached to his doctrines, in preference to all others; ascribing to him every *human* excellence; and believing he never claimed any other."

During the bitterly contested election of 1800, Jefferson had been slandered as an enemy of faith. Alexander Hamilton called him an "atheist and fanatic." With typical reserve and good taste, Jefferson refused to be lured into a game of name-calling. But that didn't stop him from being slurred. The *Gazette of the United States* intoned bombastically that voters faced a single question at the ballot box: "Shall I continue in allegiance to God—and a Religious President; Or impiously declare for Jefferson—and No God!!!" One pamphlet asked archly, "Do you believe in the strangest of all paradoxes—that a spendthrift, a libertine, or an atheist is qualified to make your laws and govern you and your posterity?" Jefferson's backers argued that their man was being skewered by Calvinist ministers eager to maintain their privileged position as the church establishment in New England—"because he is not a fanatic, nor willing that the *Quaker*, the *Baptist*, the *Methodist*, or any other denominations of Christians, should pay the pastors of other sects." New England clergy were indeed paranoid about a Jefferson administration, warning their flocks to hide their Bibles if he gained power, because the books would be confiscated.

The truth is that Jefferson read from his Bible almost every night—"I never go to bed without an hour's reading of something moral, whereon to ruminate in the intervals of sleep"—although it was his own version of the New Testament, created over the course of two or three evenings toward the end of his first term as president. *The Philosophy of Jesus of Nazareth* was assembled by cutting passages from the gospels and then rearranging them on a blank page to suit the editor's own sensibilities. Another version followed, *The Life and Morals of Jesus of Nazareth*, compiled by the same method. Both combed the gospels for texts that Jefferson felt went back to the real Jesus. He included parables like the Good Samaritan, the Prodigal Son, and discourses such as the Sermon on the Mount, as well as the trial before Pilate and crucifixion.

The tale of Jesus blessing the children, included in his *Life and Morals*, may have been among his favorites, for he was a tender parent and grandfather, and Monticello in his later years was filled with sounds of young ones. "I long to be in the midst of the children," he told daughter Martha, "and have more pleasure in their little follies than in the wisdom of the wise."

On the other hand, Jefferson's Bible omitted elements he considered fabulous, like the shepherds and angels in Bethlehem, the raising of Lazarus, Jesus walking on water and feeding the five thousand. Depictions of Christ as a sacrificial victim or divine judge were left on the cutting-room floor. How did he choose what to include? Against the fictitious dross of second-hand and second-rate materials, the authentic teachings and traditions of Jesus stood out like "diamonds in a dunghill," Jefferson maintained.

The first version of the book was purportedly created with Native Americans in mind, subtitled *"an abridgement of the New Testament for the use of the Indians, unembarrassed with matters of fact or faith beyond the level of their comprehension."* But the author's real intentions were unclear. In general, Jefferson opposed sending missionaries to "make converts" or "to change another's creed." And he held the native peoples of North America in great esteem for their unstudied eloquence. In fact, "Indians" may have been a codeword for his political opponents, who were baiting him with accusations of impiety. At any rate, he decided not to publish, because it might stir up a hornet's nest and he was "unwilling to draw on myself a swarm of insects whose buzz in more disquieting than their bite."

No resurrection narratives were included in his Bible, but that doesn't mean he had no hopes for eternity. Thomas Jefferson had known more than his share of sorrow, after all. Besides losing his father at an early age, four of his eight siblings died young. Only two of the six children from his own marriage lived to adulthood. Separation from those near and dear caused him lifelong anguish. "It is in the love of one's family that heartfelt happiness is known," he told his youngest daughter, Jane. "I feel it when we are all together and alone beyond what can be imagined."

Worst was the loss of his young wife, Martha Wayles, who died in 1782 at the age of thirty-three, occasioning a "stupor of mind" that left him immobilized and almost witless. Jefferson destroyed the personal letters they had exchanged. His love life, even more than his religion, was a private affair. But the few remaining records describe her as cheerful and trim. She had been as accomplished on the harpsichord and pianoforte as he on strings; other suitors surrendered when they heard the duets of the lovebirds courting. She was a beauty, and the rather homely swain idolized her. But after ten years of marriage, the music went out of his life. Jefferson was at her bedside for four months during her final illness; after her death, he kept to his room for weeks. A "Death Bed Adieu," a rare surviving personal effusion penned and passed on to his eldest daughter shortly before his own demise, reveals a husband yearning to rejoin his beloved in the next world:

> Life's visions are vanished, its dreams are no more,
> Dear friends of my bosom, why bathed in tears,
> I go to my fathers, I welcome the shore,
> Which crowns all my hopes, or buries my cares.

> Then farewell my dear, my loved daughter adieu,
> The last pang of life is in parting from you.
> Two seraphs await me long shrouded in death,
> I will bear them your love on my last parting breath.

But which did the grave promise—to crown human hopes or simply bury our cares? Decades after his own wife's passing, when he learned of the death of Abigail Adams, he wrote John that "I know well and feel what you have lost, what you have suffered, are suffering, and have yet to endure. The same trials have taught me that, for ills so immeasurable, time and silence are the only medicine." He prayed they might regather in an "ecstatic meeting with the friends we have loved and lost and whom we shall still love and never lose again." Adams indicated that he shared his comrade's faith, but added that if death ended all, none would be the wiser. Agreeing, Jefferson acknowledged that we really don't know what happens when we die. "The laws of nature have withheld from us knowledge of the country of spirits and left us in the dark as we were." In such cases, "the pillow of ignorance" was the softest place to lay his head.

The uncertainty never disturbed him. Whatever doubts he harbored concerning the great unknown, what mattered most was our conduct here on earth. "I am satisfied and sufficiently occupied with the things which are without tormenting or troubling myself about those which may indeed be, but of which I have no evidence," he wrote his friend in Braintree. In the end, he was sure, people would be judged by their deeds, not their creeds. "It is in our lives, and not from our words, that our religion must be read." By that measure, Thomas Jefferson surely attained a share of immortality.

From time to time, he made lists of his own notable achievements. Some of the items seem odd, like the importation of olive trees to South Carolina. The greatest benefaction any philanthropist could bestow upon his neighbors, he advised, was the introduction of a new and useful plant. But Jefferson's other deeds fill the history books. After the capital was burned in 1814, his own vast collection of books became the foundation for the nation's Library of Congress. His far-sighted acquisition of Louisiana launched the United States toward its continental reach, while his role in writing the Northwest Ordinance offered an orderly process for western lands to join the Union, as democratic states rather than second-class dominions. He abolished the laws of primogeniture and entail in Virginia and ensured that ordinary people had a chance to own and inherit land, in keeping with his vision of America as a land of small freeholders. Economic dependency bred habits of subservience, he believed, while self-reliance led to mental, as well as financial, independence.

Yet of all these achievements, he selected only three to include in his epitaph: author of the Declaration of Independence and of the Virginia Statute for Religious Freedom, and father of the University of Virginia.

Against this illustrious backdrop stands his record on slavery—the most confused and conflicted of any of the founders. Virtually none of his contemporaries envisioned an immediate extirpation of this evil. Benjamin Rush helped found the Pennsylvania Society for Promoting the Abolition of Slavery in 1774, yet believed that freed slaves would need a long period of tutelage before they could take their place as full participants in the republic. But unlike Jefferson, who favored schemes for colonizing blacks in the West, Rush was convinced that one day, at least, blacks and whites might learn to live together as members of one family. Of course, Rush himself never owned slaves. Neither did Adams, nor Paine.

Not everyone who did own them chose to remain implicated. Some, like George Washington, freed their slaves in their wills, but the more courageous did so while they were still living. In his book *Before the Mayflower*, historian Lerone Bennett calls attention to men like Philip Graham of Maryland, who freed his bondsmen, finding slavery "repugnant to the golden law of God and the unalienable right of mankind as well as to every principle of the late glorious revolution which has taken place in America." Richard Randolph, a prominent member of Virginia's landed gentry, expressed similar sentiments. On learning that he stood to inherit a sizeable plantation along with its human chattel, he declared "that I want not a single Negro for any other purpose than his immediate liberation." Edward Coles, Jefferson's own neighbor, was also born into a slave-owning family, but found it abhorrent and tried to solicit Jefferson's support for an audacious plan to take his slaves to Illinois, where he proposed to give them each 160 acres and their liberty. Coles not only carried out his ambitious scheme, but he also was eventually elected governor of Illinois, proving that one could do the right thing in the context of those times without necessarily becoming an outcast or political pariah. But Coles never did receive the support he sought from Thomas Jefferson, who stoutly condemned slavery, but continued to benefit from it throughout his life.

The same could be said of James Madison. Edward Coles was Dolley's cousin and served her husband as secretary during much of his presidency. Coles received the great man's commendation for ensuring that his former slaves received the resources needed to live as self-sufficient farmers in the Midwest. Madison wished Coles might give his freedmen a new complexion as well as a new home in Illinois, for so long as they remained dark-skinned they were likely to be ostracized socially. But Madison himself was committed to the unlikely scheme of colonizing blacks in Liberia. He promised to emancipate his slaves in his will, but faced with mounting financial difficulties (and a gambling-addicted stepson always in need of rescue) never managed it. A half dozen of Jefferson's slaves were granted freedom when their owner died, but over two hundred were sold to pay off creditors on his estate.

Many historians suggest that Jefferson was a benevolent despot toward the slaves he called his "people." But when James Hubbard, a slave who worked in the nail factory at Monticello, tried to escape to freedom, Jefferson reported that "I had him flogged in the presence of his old companions." And when the

Comte de Volney had occasion to visit Jefferson at his home in 1796, he was appalled by the "hideous and miserable semi-nudity" of the field hands; he recalled Jefferson walking among the workers with "a small whip" that he shook menacingly at those who appeared to be slacking. The Frenchman described it as "une scène comique," with the laborers working furiously under the gaze of the master, then resting idly as soon as his back was turned.

Jefferson tried to excuse his slaveholding with the assertion that blacks were childlike and incapable of caring for themselves. More than most of his contemporaries, he was the purveyor of racist caricatures. In his *Notes on the State of Virginia*, Jefferson proclaimed the black race "much inferior" in reasoning abilities to whites; in imagination he found them "dull, tasteless and anomalous." Africans, he believed, were less sensitive to heat, pain, and cold; their griefs were transient. Musically, he affirmed, they tended to be more gifted than whites, yet he doubted if they were capable of complicated harmonies. Most exuded a "very strong and disagreeable odor" and were, in his view, physically unattractive while at the same time oversexed.

Few of Jefferson's peers believed in the complete intellectual or social equality of the races, but few of them indulged in such ugly diatribes, either. When the African American poet Phillis Wheatley (ca. 1753–84) sent George Washington a lyrical tribute to celebrate his appointment as commander in chief of the Continental Army, Washington was polite enough to receive the gift as "a striking proof of your poetical talents." Jefferson, in contrast, belittled Wheatley's verses as "below the dignity of criticism."

Toward the mathematician Benjamin Banneker (1731–1806), Jefferson was more respectful. A freed slave, Banneker assisted Major Andrew Ellicott with siting surveys for the newly established capital of Washington, D.C. He taught himself astronomy and published an almanac with tables for determining the timing of eclipses and the locations of celestial bodies. Banneker sent Jefferson a copy of his ephemeris, along with a letter pleading for recognition of racial equality. "Nobody wishes more than I do to see such proofs as you exhibit that nature has given to our black brethren talents equal to those of other colors of men," Jefferson assured the autodidact, sending a copy of the computations to the Marquis de Condorcet in Paris as an instance of striking achievement:

> I am happy to be able to inform you that we have now in the United States a negro, the son of a black man born in Africa, and of a black woman born in the United States, who is a very respectable mathematician. I procured him to be employed under one of our chief directors in laying out the new federal city on the Potowmac, & in the intervals of his leisure, while on that work, he made an Almanac for the next year, which he sent me in his own handwriting, & which I inclose to you. Add to this he is a very worthy & respectable member of society.

Jefferson hoped more scientists like Banneker would emerge among his African kin "to prove that the want of talents observed in them is merely the effect of their degraded condition, and not proceeding from any difference in the structure of the parts on which intellect depends."

Few whites could calculate the orbits of comets, and a fair observer might have noted that blacks were showing themselves fully capable of equality in the field. After all, it was the African American patriot Crispus Attucks who was the first to fall in the Boston Massacre in 1770. There were blacks with Ethan Allen when he stormed Ticonderoga and with Washington when he crossed the Delaware. Ceasar Dickerson and Cuff Hayes fought with honor at Bunker Hill, and another black man was a hero that day for shooting the English Major Pitcairn when that officer popped up and announced rather prematurely, "The day is ours!" Indeed, African Americans were there at almost every major battle in the war for independence, and historians now estimate that roughly five thousand served in the Continental Army, making it the most racially diverse fighting force up until the 1950s when Harry Truman legally desegregated the military.

Few now remember the names of Lemuel Hayes, or Peter Salem, or Pomp Blackman, who fought with the Minutemen at Lexington and shouldered their muskets at Concord, but they were present—right from the beginning. And it was in that ferment of freedom that some states began to act on the radical precept that all people are endowed with inalienable rights. Vermont was the first to declare complete emancipation in 1777. Others, like Massachusetts, promised liberty to any black bondsman who was willing to enlist in the war effort. Even Georgia and South Carolina recruited black troops to serve in the cause. But not Virginia, where Thomas Jefferson was then acting governor. The only blacks who fought there did so with the Redcoats, including several hands from Monticello who fled to the British side. Jefferson signed legislation barring any freed slave from residing in Virginia, much less carrying a gun.

His denunciations of slavery mostly came to naught. A clause he proposed for the Virginia Constitution would have banned the importation of slaves to his home state, but the measure was rejected. His original draft of the Declaration of Independence indicted George III for encouraging the slave trade in the colonies—a commerce he described as "a cruel war against human nature itself"—but the words were deleted from the final document. John Quincy Adams caught the contradiction nicely: Thomas Jefferson "abhorred slavery from his soul" and yet "left slavery precisely where it was."

In extenuation, Jefferson never ceased to admit that slavery was not only wrong, but a monstrous crime and folly. Temperamentally, he was an optimist who hoped that later generations might find a resolution to the iniquity his own generation was unwilling to confront. Theologically, he lacked any strong awareness of evil. But slavery came as close as anything to stirring his personal sense of sin. Unlike later generations of slaveholders, who cultivated the self-serving myth that slavery was a benign institution, Jefferson recognized that "the whole commerce between master and slave is a perpetual exercise of the most boisterous passions, the most unremitting despotism on the one part, and degrading submissions on the other." The system dehumanized everyone it touched, and "the man must be a prodigy who can retain his manners and morals undepraved by such circumstances." Jefferson's first memory, from the time he was two or three years old, was of being carried upon a pillow in the arms of a black servant. His own finely tuned sense of right and wrong was warped from a lifetime of unearned privilege. But he always felt uneasy about his complicity and believed the nation would eventually be judged guilty, too:

Indeed I tremble for my country when I reflect that God is just; that his justice cannot sleep forever; that considering numbers, nature and natural means only, a revolution of the wheel of fortune, an exchange of situation, is among possible events: that it may become probable by supernatural interference. The Almighty has no attribute which can take side with us in such a contest.

Here Thomas Jefferson sounds less like a philosopher discussing abstract theories of natural rights than like a Hebrew prophet pronouncing judgment on the nations. Freedom was not merely a good idea; for Jefferson, it was a divine mandate. He combined the ideals of the Enlightenment with the fire of a moral crusader—thunder as well as light.

Perhaps the most perceptive man ever elected president, he had the biggest moral blind spots also. And the nation founded on his premise that "all men are created equal" still struggles with the unfinished business of the Revolution he helped to start.

9.

The Dictates of Conscience

The Faith of James Madison

Shortly before he died, Thomas Jefferson entrusted his political and spiritual legacy to his closest collaborator, James Madison. "To myself you have been a pillar of support thro' life. Take care of me when dead, and be assured that I shall leave you with my last affections." They had known each other for half a century, having met in the momentous year of 1776, and while Madison initially looked to the older man as a mentor, Jefferson would come to call his friend "the greatest man in the world." One articulated the ideal of American independence; the other engineered the reality of national self-government.

"Mr. Jefferson has more imagination and passion, quicker and richer conceptions," recounted one eyewitness. "Mr. Madison has a sound judgment, tranquil temper and logical mind," and was perhaps the more profound of the two. The eight years that separated the duo were little compared to the bonds they shared: books and ideas, gracious manners and revolutionary instincts. Madison's Montpelier, the manse that commanded an extensive view of the Blue Ridge Mountains, was just twenty-five miles from Monticello, constructed on a similar Palladian design and furnished with ornate doors, fine flooring, and hardware imported from France, surrounded by several thousand acres of rich red Piedmont farmland still mottled thickly with stands of virgin timber. Madison recalled that his ancestors were "planters and among the respectable though not the most opulent class," but he and Jefferson, along with other slave owners like George Washington, James Monroe, and Patrick Henry (distantly related to both James and Dolley) were among the two or three hundred families—many bound through intermarriage—who dominated the politics of the colony of Virginia. As gentry, they lived with a sense of entitlement, but also noblesse oblige.

Like Jefferson, "Jemmy" was reared an Anglican, baptized by the Reverend William Davis of the Hanover Parish Church when he was just fifteen days old on Sunday, March 31, 1751. His father was on the vestry of the Brick Church, another house of worship, constructed six or seven miles distant from the family home when Jemmy was still a youngster. But being a vestryman was not necessarily a mark of spiritual ardor in those days—quite the contrary.

Decadence characterized Virginia's entire religious establishment, not least the vestries, which were filled with wealthy planters. These magnates were accustomed to a lifestyle of ease—and to having things their own way. Along with administering the poor funds, they were charged with supervising their local parish priests, meaning they could dock or dismiss any parson who stepped out of line. Clerics who chided their flocks for trading horses on a Sunday, dueling with pistols, or other unchristian habits might find their jobs in jeopardy. The archbishop of Canterbury complained that Virginia vestries hired and fired their pastors like "domestic servants," circumventing the bishop's authority to impose discipline. Reports of drunkenness and indolence among the priesthood were common. Intermingling church and state led to worldliness in pew and pulpit. Thus William Byrd, a contemporary who eventually rose to the governor's council, listed "vestryman" in his memoirs as his first elective office—merely one stepping-stone in a long political career. But unlike Byrd, James Madison Sr. gave every appearance of being devout in his faith. So did the son, at least in the beginning.

His first teacher was Donald Robertson, an able schoolmaster and licensed preacher educated in Aberdeen and the University of Edinburgh. Enrolled as a boarder in the master's academy in King and Queen County at age eleven, the pupil quickly became proficient in Latin and Greek. Jemmy also acquired some fluency in French, which he learned to inflect with a broad Scots accent. (After graduating, he loved to tell of his attempts to converse with a French visitor, to whom he might as well have been speaking Kickapoo.) In addition to languages, algebra, geometry, and geography were included in the curriculum, while a "Book of Logick" in Madison's hand preserves youthful lessons in the use and abuse of syllogism:

1. No sinners are happy;
2. Angels are happy; therefore
3. Angels are not sinners.

Not all the illustrations were so edifying. ("You are an animal; a goose is an animal; therefore you are a goose.") What Madison took away from such lessons, intended to teach valid and fallacious forms of reasoning, was a lasting respect for precise, analytical argument over pretty turns of speech.

Moral instruction came largely from literature. A commonplace book from his school days contains maxims for living copied from authors both classical and modern. From Montaigne: "A man should not delight in praises that are not his due." And from the Abbé du Bos: "Nothing makes one say and commit so many silly things as the desire to appear witty," an adage the youth may have taken too seriously. While Madison developed an off-color sense of humor, jocularity was never his trademark.

Natural philosophy made a lasting impression. At Robertson's school, young Madison penned a diagram titled "The Solar System from Copernicus," showing planets ranging from Mercury to Saturn, surrounded by their respective satellites and accompanied by each object's distance from the sun. Other sketches include plans for constructing a sundial, computing the angles of inclination and "hour lines" to tell time at latitude 38°N, near his home. Years later, at the Constitutional Convention, John Dickinson of Delaware used an astronomical analogy to describe the functioning of the proposed federal system: "Let our central government be like the sun, and the states the planets, repelled yet attracted, and the whole moving regularly and harmoniously in their separate orbits." Madison also pondered how, like a good government, "the planetary system is regulated by fixed laws and presents a scene of order and proportion," lessons he learned early on. Though he was tutored at home for another two years before heading to college, the quality of education Madison encountered with his Scots schoolmaster was unsurpassed: "All that I have been in my life I owe largely to that man."

Studies at Princeton followed. Then called the College of New Jersey, the university had been founded to train clergy for the Presbyterian ministry. Morning prayers began at 6:00 a.m. with an exposition of scripture. Evening devotions were at five in the afternoon, when students took turns singing psalms. Piety prevailed. The rules regulating campus life were intended "to direct the conduct and studies of the youth; and to restrain them from such liberties and indulgences as would tend to corrupt their morals, or alienate their minds from a steady application." Proctors maintained steady watch. Nassau Hall, where students lodged, kept its inmates "sequestered from the various temptations, attending a promiscuous converse with the world, that theatre of folly and dissipation." Naturally, college pranks proliferated: "Meeting and Shoving in the dark entries; Knocking at Doors and going off without entering; freezing the Bell; Ringing it late Hours of the Night" and even "Parading bad Women" along with contests in the composition of bawdy poetry, at which Madison excelled. Such amusements rarely drew heavy penalties from authorities, who tried to steer a middle course between "too great a licentiousness on the one hand, or an excessive precision on the other."

For a religious bastion, the intellectual atmosphere at Princeton was surprisingly liberal. Students of all denominations were invited to enroll. Though the president, John Witherspoon, was a thoroughgoing Presbyterian, he had a long history of opposing church establishments in Scotland and was personally committed to "a right to private judgment in matters of opinion." At least in theory, theological errors at Princeton were not to be suppressed, but rather countered through open debate. At graduation exercises in 1770, Mathias Williamson upheld the proposition that "Every religious Profession, which does not by its Principles disturb the public Peace, ought to be tolerated by a wise State," while the college president's own son gave a rousing Latin defense of the precept that natural law requires defiance to tyrannical kings. Students including Madison followed the unfolding schism with Britain. John Hancock was a graduation speaker, and Witherspoon himself went on to sign the Declaration of Independence (the only clergyman to do so). While the reverend dominated the school through the force of his personality, therefore, the thrust of his teaching was to question authority, whether royal or ecclesiastical. "In the instruction of the youth," Princeton's stated goal was not to indoctrinate but to "cherish a spirit of liberty, and free enquiry."

At this stage, Jemmy did not push the limits of inquiry very far. His thoughts were dominated by the awareness of mortality. All his life, he suffered from poor health. He wasn't a little man; at five feet six inches he was as tall as Aaron Burr, and just an inch shorter than Alexander Hamilton, so about average for the time. But he was physically delicate, subject to incapacitating spells resembling epileptic seizures. With sandy hair cut in bangs and pale complexion, he seemed immature for his years.

His decision to attend Princeton was prompted partly by caution. The tidewater area where the College of William and Mary was located was regarded as "unfavorable to the health of persons from the mountainous region." Princeton was also undoubtedly the better school since William Small—Jefferson's preceptor at William and Mary—had returned to England. But mental and bodily stress mounted in New Jersey, where the student managed to compress the usual four years of study into two by depriving himself of sleep. Eyestrain from poring over his books—Madison was near-sighted in one eye and far-sighted in the other, with such poor vision that he had difficulty shaving himself in a mirror—contributed to the problem. At the end of the ordeal, Madison complained of vague "sensations" that "intimated to me not to expect a long or healthy life."

Physical collapse precipitated a spiritual crisis. Many young graduates wonder what to do with their lives after college. For a serious-minded individual whose customary enjoyments were "Solitude and Contemplation," the aristocratic dissipations of drinking and gaming that occupied other well-born Virginians were obviously out of the question. Madison's struggle was exacerbated by intimations that his years might be brief. Expecting an early grave, he was disinclined "to set about anything that is difficult in acquiring and useless in possessing after one has exchanged Time for Eternity." Military service was impossible. Though briefly commissioned in the Orange County militia, he lacked the stamina for drills. Was ministry an option? Corresponding with William Bradford, another Princeton graduate struggling to find his niche, Madison warned that "a watchful eye must be kept on ourselves lest while we are building ideal monuments of Renown and Bliss here we neglect to have our names enrolled in the Annals of

Heaven." A priestly calling was alluring, since "a divine may be the most useful as well as the most happy member of society." Madison began reading and making notations on scriptural commentaries and briefly took up the study of Hebrew. A prayer book for leading family devotions also survives from this period. But even a clergyman's duties seemed strenuous beyond imagining, while the prospect of weekly preaching petrified the future statesman. He didn't have the stained-glass voice or the temperament.

Madison was shy in public and in lengthy discourse could drop his remarks to a whisper. He didn't like the spotlight, and much of his later work—like ghostwriting George Washington's Inaugural Address, then penning the formal reply of Congress—was done behind the scenes. Fortunately, politicians of that era didn't need to be good on the stump. All that was required for a man like Madison to gain elective office was a hint that he would be willing to serve. So when Jemmy finally decided to study law, it was never with the intention of litigating or pleading cases before the bench. Rather he sought to acquaint himself with the "Origin and fundamental principles of Legislation." Statecraft was his aim. Writing again to Bradford, the aspiring scholar sounded a little diffident about the prospect. "The principles and Modes of Government are too important to be disregarded by an Inquisitive mind and I think are well worthy of a critical examination by all students that have health and Leisure." But with America marching double-time toward open revolt, the time for leisurely detachment was over. Colonial legislatures hurried to create constitutions to replace the ad hoc networks of Committees of Safety that had been coordinating resistance to Britain. As a newly elected member of the Virginia Convention in 1776, Madison discovered the task that would occupy him for the next sixty years: creating the structures of governance to sustain a free society.

Religious liberty was especially dear to his heart. When the Virginia Company was chartered in 1606, its mission was to bring "Christian religion to such people as yet live in darkness and miserable ignorance of the true knowledge and worship of God." Early statutes made denying the Trinity a capital crime; casting derision on "God's holy word" was also punishable by death. Catholics were forbidden to hold public office, while "popish priests" were immediately deported, as were Quakers. Citizens were required to sustain the Anglican establishment with their taxes and expected to attend services regularly. While Madison was still at Princeton, Baptist preachers were being stoned out of Culpepper County in his home state and imprisoned in Spotsylvania for preaching without a permit. It infuriated him.

Despite the religious establishment in Virginia—or because of it—heartfelt piety languished while "Poverty and luxury prevail among all sorts; pride, ignorance, and knavery among the priesthood, and vice and wickedness among the laity." Madison became committed to the complete uncoupling of church and state, as much to foster a more deeply held faith among the majority as to check the religious persecution of minorities.

His first act in the Virginia Convention was to amend the Declaration of Rights, the philosophical foreword to the state's new Constitution. An initial statement crafted by George Mason promised Virginians "fullest Toleration in the Exercise of Religion," certainly an advance for harassed groups like the Baptists, but still not enough. A government with the power to issue edicts of "toleration" for certain sects could just as easily claim the authority to regulate or restrict them. Like Thomas Paine—whom he would befriend when others had abandoned the aging radical—James Madison understood that "Toleration is not the opposite of intolerance, but is the counterfeit of it. Both are despotisms. The one assumes to itself the right of withholding liberty of conscience, the other of granting it." Madison was successful in altering the "fullest Toleration in the Exercise of Religion" to "the free exercise of religion" so that the final article read:

> That religion, or the duty which we owe our Creator, and the manner of discharging it, can be directed only by reason and conviction, not by force and violence; and therefore, all men are equally entitled to the free exercise of religion, according to the dictates of conscience. . . .

The principle had been enunciated: every person possessed religious liberty, not at the sufferance of a tolerant state, but as a natural right. Partisans of a tax-supported church were down but not out.

It was at this point that James Madison met Thomas Jefferson. In the next session of the convention, the two served together on a Committee on Religion. And as partners, they would go on nine years later to completely eliminate the Anglican establishment in Virginia. Patrick Henry in 1784 proposed giving state incorporation to the Episcopal Church and levying a general assessment to support "teachers of the Christian religion." To many, the bill appeared benign; dissenters were exempt from underwriting the salaries of clergy they repudiated. Washington straddled, telling George Mason he wasn't in principle opposed to "making people pay towards the support of that which they profess," while warning that Henry's measure might be "impolitic." But Baptists, Methodists, Presbyterians, and others outside the official establishment remembered the harsh treatment they'd received before the Revolution. By the thousands, they signed Madison's 1785 reply to Patrick Henry, the Memorial and Remonstrance Against Religious Assessments, protesting the notion that "the Civil Magistrate is a competent Judge of Religious truth."

No one questioned that religion made for a healthy society. The issue was whether government support was necessary or healthy for religion. History said no. Madison wrote:

> Because experience witnesseth that ecclesiastical establishments, instead of maintaining the purity and efficacy of Religion, have had a contrary operation. During almost fifteen centuries, has the legal establishment of Christianity been on trial. What have been its fruits?

The church was at its best in the early years, following the death of its founder, when the disciples of Jesus were a persecuted and powerless minority. When Christianity became the official religion of the Roman Empire under Constantine, and later in the medieval world, organized religion became an enclave of "superstition, bigotry, and persecution." Madison's arguments proved persuasive, and Henry's bill was defeated.

The Memorial and Remonstrance struck a chord with the changing population of Virginia. As increasing numbers of dissenters settled along the frontier, Anglicans were no longer the numerical majority. And responding to popular demand, the General Assembly the following year passed Thomas Jefferson's Statute for Religious Freedom, which finally voided

Virginia's establishment altogether. The older man considered it one of the capstones of his career, but Madison deserves enormous credit for pushing the bill through the legislature while its author was in France.

Two years later, in 1787, Madison was instrumental in organizing the Constitutional Convention and, by securing Washington's participation, ensuring it had clout to get the job done. Benjamin Franklin was there, too, to inspire delegates to the grandeur of their mission. Called for the ostensible purpose of regulating commerce, the convention had larger aims. Everyone knew the Articles of Confederation were ineffectual. The central government needed more power, but not too much power, and that was the catch. Authority also had to be restrained within wholesome limits. Perhaps remembering his syllogisms from Mr. Robertson's academy, Madison made the dilemma plain:

> If men were angels, no government would be necessary. If angels were to govern men, neither external nor internal controls on government would be necessary. In framing a government which is to be administered by men over men, the great difficulty lies in this: You must first enable the government to control the governed; and in the next place, oblige it to control itself.

The "Virginia Plan" Madison developed became the template for the United States Constitution, based on three separate and coequal branches of government, with the idea that "each may be a check on the other." The Bill of Rights, likewise bearing Madison's stamp, offered an extra layer of protection against government encroachment. In addition to these internal controls, the United States by its very size and variety would keep any one ideological faction from dominating the rest. "In a free government the security for civil rights must be the same as that for religious rights," Madison proposed. "It consists in the one case in the multiplicity of interests, and in the other case in the multiplicity of sects."

Conventional thinking said that religious uniformity made for order and tranquility, but Madison disagreed. Enforced homogeneity was smothering and bred unrest. Recalling Voltaire's maxim that the existence of only one religion in a nation produces slavery and two ignites civil war, while a multitude produces peace, Madison made spiritual diversity the linchpin of American liberty.

Jemmy had come a long way since his college days. He had found vital and vitalizing work. During Washington's first term, he was at the president's right hand, his counsel sought over every point for how the newly minted government should function. There were a hundred questions to be answered, from the etiquette of how the chief executive should be addressed ("Mister President" rather than more exalted titles) to cabinet appointments. Though Madison continued to suffer from a "bilious" disposition, breakdowns like those of former days would never again produce the same existential jitters. Nor would he post any more thoughts of trading time for eternity. Apparently, he had turned a corner, vocationally and mentally. Naturally, historians have asked whether the prayerful preoccupations of his youth were also a passing phase.

Madison appeared to gravitate toward Deism as he matured, falling under the spell of natural religion. In the spring of 1791, with the Constitution ratified and the government up and running, he felt well enough to undertake an extended trip through the north country with his friend Thomas Jefferson. Embarking from New York up the Hudson, the two spent the better part of a month traversing the Adirondacks and Vermont before heading south through the Berkshires and Connecticut, traveling by horseback, canoe, and sailing sloop. In early June, they lodged in Bennington with Vermont's Governor Moses Robinson, who invited them to worship at the local Congregational parish that Sunday morning. Asked afterward how they enjoyed the music, the two travelers responded that they had no basis for comparison, since neither had been to church in many years.

The journey was a botanic expedition, Jefferson recording "rich groves of Thuja, silver fir, white pine, aspen and paper birch" along with New England's famous sugar maples, Madison remarking on the farming methods and soil conditions. After weeks of communing with the great outdoors, Jefferson noted that his companion was tired but "in better health than I have seen him."

Both were avid students of natural history, but more of their research was undertaken in books rather than in the field. The theories of Georges-Louis Leclerc, known as Comte de Buffon, came in for special scrutiny. Madison possessed over fifty of Buffon's works, on topics ranging from probability and number theory, astronomy and optics, to physics. But Buffon, a mathematical genius, was best known for his thirty-six-volume *Histoire naturelle*, where he developed his theories of geology and biology, including the origins of life. There he proposed that the Earth and other planets had come into existence in a long-ago cataclysm when a comet struck the sun, sending stellar debris shooting into space. The Earth that formed out of this astral collision was extremely hot at first. But over the millennia—Buffon postulated a period of at least 74,000 years was required, although he admitted that it might have taken millions—the planet cooled. As temperatures dropped, water condensed into liquid form. Oceans appeared. And heat acting on naturally occurring substances in the depths of the sea spawned the first living creatures.

The theory was remarkable for suggesting that life originated without divine intervention and for introducing "deep time" into the study of earth science. Most educated Americans in the eighteenth century still held to a biblical chronology of creation. Ezra Stiles, the president of Yale from 1778 to 1795, remembered calculating while riding to school as a boy "that God had made the world 5,700 years before. Looking at the great cliff of East Rock as he rode into New Haven, he could be sure the Deluge had washed over it exactly 4,032 years ago in the time of Noah." But enlightened thinkers had begun to question the biblical account. In his *Notes on the State of Virginia*, for instance, Jefferson had noticed that at least seventy-four species of quadrupeds were found only in America, including raccoons, skunks, and opossums. The birds of America were also quite different than those of Europe. If all had been passengers aboard the Ark, why were some animals found on just one continent? "My opinion of this story," chuckled Tom Paine, "is the same as what a man once said to another, who asked him in a drawling tone of voice, 'Do you believe the account about No-ah?' The other replied in the same tone of voice, *ah-no*." Neither Madison nor Jefferson credited the fable of the flood, either.

Theories of a universal deluge were popular, not only among churchmen. Fossilized shells had been found high in the mountains, from the Alps to the Andes. Closer to home, sea coal and mineralized cockleshells were plentiful in Virginia's own Blue Ridge, and to some naturalists the impressions of marine organisms in such locations confirmed the Bible's claim that the globe had once been covered in water. How else account for such anomalies? In his first edition of *Notes on the State of Virginia*, published in Paris, Jefferson ventured the fossils might be chemical accretions rather than biological in origin, but after criticism from creationists, he dropped that hypothesis. In future printings, he alluded to three possible explanations. Calculating the impossible weight and volume of water necessary to cover the planet to an altitude of fifteen thousand feet above sea level, the highest elevations where shells occurred, as well as the difficulties in disposing of such a flood through evaporation, he dismissed the theory of any general inundation. He likewise rejected the explanation geologists would favor today, that ancient sea beds had been thrust upward long ago, since no operative seismic forces known at that time could produce such stupendous results. The third suggestion he credited to Voltaire, who had observed the spontaneous production of shells in metamorphic stone. "From this fact, I suppose, he would have us infer, that, besides the usual process for generating shells by the elaboration of earth and water in animal vessels, nature may have provided an equivalent operation, by passing the same materials through the pores of calcareous earths." But this violated the principle of economy, for nature seldom used two separate mechanisms to achieve a single end. Withholding judgment, Jefferson conceded that "the three hypotheses are equally unsatisfactory; and we must be contented to acknowledge, that this great phaenomenon is as yet unsolved. Ignorance is preferable to error; and he is less remote from truth who believes nothing, then he who believes what is wrong."

Madison and Jefferson were alike intrigued by the puzzle of Earth's origins. The man from Monticello admitted that geology was not his best subject. While recommending its study as useful for learning "the ordinary arrangement of the different strata of minerals in the earth, to know from their habitual collocations, and proximities, where we find one mineral; where another, for which we are seeking," by life's end he almost gave up on gaining any grand insights into the world's formation. "Dreams about the modes of creation, enquiries whether our globe has been formed by the agency of fire or water, how many millions of years it has cost Vulcan or Neptune to produce what the fiat of the Creator would effect by a single act of will, is too idle to be worth a single hour of any man's life." Yet he himself spent many hours on such inquiries and never gave credence to a "young Earth." More than once, the philosophically minded statesman pondered what forces might have conspired to sculpt the natural bridge near his home—whether a "great convulsion" (as suggested in his *Notes*) or the slow, steady friction of water on rock (the conclusion he eventually embraced). Overlooking the confluence of the Potomac and Shenandoah rivers, he conjectured that "this earth has been created in time, that the mountains were formed first, that the rivers began to flow afterward, that in this place, particularly, they have been dammed up by the Blue Ridge of mountains, and have formed an ocean which filled the whole valley; that continuing to rise they have at length broken over at this spot, and have torn the mountain down from its summit to its base." But how many lifetimes had it required for the mountain to be built and then demolished? On such questions he retreated into agnosticism. "I myself am an emperic in natural philosophy, suffering my faith to go no farther than my facts."

Madison shared his older friend's curiosity, along with his passion for empirical data, and the two corresponded extensively about how Buffon's theory that Earth was born in a fireball could be tested. Madison proposed the oblate shape of the Earth might yield measurements to confirm that the planet was cooling from the core. Based on "the calculations of Martin grounded on the data of Maupertuis," a French astronomer, the diameter of the Earth was 89.8 miles longer at the equator than at the poles. This meant the polar regions were effectively 45 miles closer to the molten center of the planet than the equatorial zones. At least in theory, Madison suggested, there should be "a discoverable difference in the degrees of heat emitted" as one shifted latitude south to north across the Earth's surface.

To determine the age of the Earth, it never would have occurred to either of the men to consult the book of Genesis or tomes of theology. How the solar system formed, how life began and evolved—these were questions to be answered through observation and experiment rather than through special revelation.

Anticipating Darwin, Buffon had asked, "At what distance from man shall we place the great apes, which resemble him so perfectly in bodily conformation? Were all the species of animals formerly what they are today?" In response, the Frenchman proposed that the cooling Earth forced vast migrations in ancient times—explaining, for instance, why the fossil remains of elephants were found in Siberia, while the animal's modern descendants lived only in the tropics—and that during the course of these migrations a kind of paraevolution took place. Without exactly changing species, animals modified their internal and external features to suit their altered habitat. Madison undertook a series of dissections to throw light on this hypothesis, comparing the morphology of small mammals in North America with those of South America and Europe. He took thirty-three careful measurements of a female weasel, sending the results along with the skins of several other quadrupeds to Jefferson in Paris, receiving in return two boxes of chemical supplies along with an introductory textbook to satisfy "a little itch to gain a smattering in chymistry."

In acknowledgment of Madison's growing scientific stature, the American Philosophical Society inducted him into membership in 1785, along with Joseph Priestley and Thomas Paine.

One is known by the company one keeps. According to the Reverend William Meade, bishop of the Episcopal Church in Virginia, Madison's "political associations with those of infidel principles, of whom there were many in his day, if they did not actually change his creed, yet subjected him to the general suspicion of it." A fellow Princeton graduate, Meade had only one personal encounter with James Madison—which obviously left the clergyman somewhat shaken:

> I was never at Mr. Madison's but once, and then our conversation took such a turn—although not designed on my part—as to call forth some expressions and arguments which left the impression on my mind that his creed was not strictly regulated by the Bible.

James Madison was always outwardly respectful of religious formalities, Meade reported, attending worship and occasionally inviting ministers to his home. "Whatever may have been the private sentiments of Mr. Madison on the subject of religion, he was never known to declare any hostility to it."

His private sentiments are difficult to determine, for in his later years, he rarely mentioned matters of faith. He clearly believed in a Creator. Supposing the world had existed forever, with no beginning, merely pushed the mystery of origins into infinite regress. For Madison, the universe must have had some First Cause, and it was easier to imagine "an invisible cause possessing infinite power, wisdom and goodness" than to imagine the universe "visibly destitute of those attributes." The cosmos didn't just make itself, in other words—an intelligence was behind it.

But was this Nature's God or the Holy One of Christian scriptures? A letter to Frederick Beasley from 1825 affirmed that belief in God "is so essential to the moral order of the World and to the happiness of man, that arguments which enforce it cannot be drawn from too many sources." But with a nod to Beasley's abstract "proofs" of the deity, Madison suggested that reasoning "from Nature to Nature's God" was the best way to think about divinity. To Dr. Charles Caldwell the following year, he expressed similar sentiments. Receiving from the doctor a pamphlet on phrenology, Madison replied that he saw nothing foolish in the theory that specific mental functions might be localized in particular areas of the brain. Heartened by the "politeness and liberality" of this response, Caldwell then sent the former president a religious tract that had drawn fire from "the ultra-theological orthodox." Madison replied:

I concur with you at once in rejecting the idea maintained by some divines of more zeal than discretion that there is no road from nature up to Nature's God, and that all the knowledge of his existence and attributes which preceded the written revelation of them, was derived from oral tradition.

The Creator might be known directly from his handiwork, in other words, with or without the benefit of scripture. Though Madison acknowledged the fallibility of human reasoning—particularly when pondering the imponderable—still there were no substitutes for facts or clear-witted thinking. He was at home with natural religion: a deity directly accessible, through reason and everyday experience.

Deism is frequently portrayed as a cold and disembodied faith, worshiping a watchmaker God, but that was not how it appeared to thinkers like Madison. Rather, it was the God of Noah who seemed recondite and inapproachable—mired in myth, awash in the antediluvian speculations of prelates like Bishop Ussher (1581–1656), who calculated the Almighty had begun his work on October 26, 4004, BC, at nine in the morning. By contrast, Nature's God was sensible and almost sensuous: incontrovertible as gravity and gracious as the falling rain.

The founders' view of Creation was never mechanical or without a spiritual dimension. Holding that "the life of the husbandman is pre-eminently suited to the comfort and happiness of the individual," Madison retained lifelong enthusiasm for farming and even as president retreated regularly from the White House to the rolling hills of Montpelier, to be mentally refreshed and inwardly renewed. Earth was a verdant field, a goodly habitation, not just a venue for taxonomic classification. His spirituality was rooted in love of nature and the soil.

What happened to the Christian convictions of his youth? When James Madison did attend church, it continued to be in the Anglican tradition. But that tradition was in ferment. Following the Revolution, Americans distanced themselves from the Church of England. Prayers for the king and royal family were naturally eliminated from the liturgy. But many in the newly founded Protestant Episcopal Church of the United States wanted even bigger changes in their modes of worship. A proposed United States Book of Common Prayer from 1786, for example, would have erased any mention of hell and dispensed with the suggestion in the baptismal rite that human beings are born in sin. The Athanasian Creed, a Trinitarian statement in use since the sixth century, would have been omitted as well. Some congregations, like King's Chapel in Boston, left the Anglican fold entirely and became openly Unitarian at this time. And although the changes proposed in 1786 were finally rejected—conservatives carried the day—Madison seemed in sympathy with the innovators. When George Ticknor of Harvard visited with Madison some years later, he found the president "curious to know how the cause of liberal Christianity stood with us, and if the Athanasian creed was well received by our Episcopalians. He pretty distinctly intimated to me his own regard for the Unitarian doctrines."

Like nearly all the founders, Madison admired Jesus's teachings of love to God and neighbor. But like his mentor Thomas Jefferson, another nominal Episcopalian, he may have harbored doubts about Christ's wonder-working and claims to divinity. Dolley's niece Mary Cutts said her uncle "though no sectarian, was a religious man" who accepted the "religion of the Bible and of the heart." Did embracing the "religion of the Bible" mean that he rejected later add-ons like the doctrine of God in three persons? We can only guess, since Madison never elaborated on these tenets.

Shortly after his eightieth birthday, he sketched out a brief autobiography, but unlike gossipy memoirs today, it contained no confessions or untold secrets, only a modest outline of his public achievements. In keeping with his wishes, his intimate notes and papers were destroyed after his death. And this says a good deal about his attitude toward faith. Whatever he really believed was a transaction between him and the ultimate. Religion belonged to the private realm of conscience, beyond the scrutiny of curiosity seekers or officious busybodies.

Conscience was sacrosanct, to be safeguarded at all costs. As architect of the Bill of Rights, Madison had compiled the first ten amendments by sifting through suggestions generated at the various state conventions to ratify the Constitution. But he also made proposals of his own. One amendment (never adopted) would have exempted conscientious objectors from military service. Another would have extended federal guarantees of religious liberty to the states. Protecting the individual's right to worship freely—and to dissent from the mainstream—was paramount.

As president, Madison remained determined to keep government at arm's length from organized religion. During the War of 1812, he broke this rule by proclaiming a national day of prayer, inviting all who were "piously disposed" to give thanks to "the Great Parent and Sovereign of the Universe." But the supplication was worded so generically that a disgruntled "Bible Christian" was unable to discover a single phrase "which could be offensive to the ear of a pagan, an infidel, a deist, and scarcely to that of an atheist." And of course that is the problem with presidential prayers and other expressions of official sanctity—they are bound to offend somebody. By the end of his life, Madison regretted issuing the prayer at all. His faith was an intensely personal concern.

Was that what made him so compatible with Dolley? Theirs was a midlife marriage. James was forty-three and a bachelor. Dolley was seventeen years younger and previously married, her first husband and newborn child having perished in the terrible contagion of yellow fever that decimated Philadelphia in 1793, leaving her with another son not quite two. Her Quaker family had moved there when she was fourteen, freeing their slaves and quitting the South for a community where the children might grow up among Friends. Twenty years before he proposed, Madison had praised Quaker Pennsylvania for its "liberal, catholic and equitable way of thinking as to the rights of conscience." Yet the Friends could be hidebound, too. Dolley was ejected from the meeting for marrying outside the faith, "before a hireling priest."

In many ways, they were opposites. Unlike her quiet husband, Dolley was sociable and a vivacious hostess. After the informality of the Jefferson administration, Madison's White House years set new standards for entertaining. Dolley became famous for her Wednesday levees, formal presidential receptions she made fashionable. Having dressed so plainly as a girl, she was notorious for her turbans and daring necklines, whereas James's costume was consistently dull. One associate said he had never seen Mr. Madison in any color other than black. James preferred chess, while Dolley liked cards. But over the years, like any happily wed couple, they came to resemble one another. In retirement, the two occasionally ran foot races with each other, and Dolley more than kept up. Observing the pair after four decades of marriage, a perceptive English visitor described her as "a strong-minded woman, fully capable of entering into her husband's occupations and cares; and there is little doubt that he owed much to her intellectual companionship." Spiritually they converged. James studied the teachings of George Fox, and after spending most of her life as a Quaker—for even when expelled by the Friends, she still held to her inner light—Dolley finally joined St. John's Episcopal parish. Shared values gave them a common center of gravity—stars in synchronous orbit.

Keeping his pledge to care for Thomas Jefferson's legacy, Madison in his eighth decade took over as rector for the University of Virginia. "It is a comfort to leave that institution under your care," sighed his friend. Like the school's founder, Madison believed that learning was "the best security against crafty and dangerous encroachments on the public liberty," and the two had labored together since 1816 to make the university a nonsectarian center for higher education. According to the original scheme, the curriculum was to include ancient and modern languages, mathematics, physics, chemistry, biology, anatomy and medicine, government and humanities. No divinity school was contemplated. In response to protests that the school was irreligious, accommodations were made for various denominations to set up private seminaries on grounds adjacent to the campus, where Jefferson hoped that "by bringing the sects together and mixing them with the mass of other students, we shall soften their asperities, liberalize and neutralize their prejudices, and make the general religion a religion of peace, reason and morality." All faiths might have access to the library, and Madison was asked to draw up a bibliography of books on theology for the collection. The catalogue he compiled was eclectic. It included the Bible, but also the Qur'an; Luther and Calvin, but also the heretic Socinus; Cotton Mather and Jonathan Edwards, but also John Locke, Richard Price, and Joseph Priestley. Books, like opinions, ought to be multifarious.

By the end of his life, James had the satisfaction of seeing the last religious monopolies in America crumble. Several colonies—Rhode Island, New Jersey, Pennsylvania, Delaware—had embraced religious freedom from their very inception. And in the aftermath of the Revolution, the rather anemic Anglican establishments in New York, Maryland, Georgia, and the Carolinas collapsed of their own accord. Those New England states that were the legatees of Puritanism were the last holdouts. New Hampshire maintained tax support for its religious establishment until 1817 and Connecticut until 1818. Maine liberalized its laws in 1820, while Massachusetts, the final bulwark, fell thirteen years later. The free exercise of religion had replaced "toleration" throughout the nation.

By that time, most of the founding fathers were gone. Except for Madison, the other participants from the Constitutional Convention were all deceased, and Charles Carroll, the last signer of the Declaration of Independence, passed away in 1832. Madison's thoughts must have turned to life's transience and to what abides, for that same year he wrote that man's nature appears to contain an "anticipation of his future existence." Whatever his exact beliefs about the world to come, he probably sensed that his life's purpose here was complete.

In 1836, as the sixtieth anniversary of the signing of the Declaration of Independence approached, Madison's strength ebbed. His presidential successor James Monroe had died on Independence Day five years earlier, maintaining the grand precedent set by John Adams and Thomas Jefferson, and many urged James Madison to hang on until the Fourth of July, to make a patriotic exit.

But he departed on his own timetable. Years before, Jefferson had discussed the prospect of assisted suicide using an extract of the *Datura stramonium* or jimsonweed which "brings on the sleep of death as quietly as fatigue does the ordinary sleep, without the least struggle or motion." It was much preferable to the Greeks' hemlock or the Romans' technique of slitting a vein, in his opinion. Could such a medication be restrained to self-administration, Jefferson urged "it ought not to be kept secret. There are ills in life as desperate as intolerable, to which it would be the rational relief, e.g. the inveterate cancer." Whether or not Madison fully agreed, he refused stimulants and other life-prolonging medicines that might have extended his span the six days needed to reach the Fourth. Having spent his life in defense of individual liberties, he exercised his own right to self-determination in the end.

On June 27, his last full day on earth, he spent several hours dictating a thank-you note to Professor George Tucker, whose biography of Thomas Jefferson had just been dedicated to him. The older man had been dead for a decade, and Madison epitomized their fifty years of friendship: "A sincere and stead-fast co-operation in promoting such a reconstruction of our political system as would provide for the permanent liberty and happiness of the United States." That liberty was grounded in the separation of church and state. Freedom of religion was the cause that excited Madison's best energies and elicited his most brilliant advocacy, from the Memorial and Remonstrance to the United States Constitution and First Amendment.

At breakfast the next morning, his niece Nelly noticed her uncle having some difficulty swallowing and asked if anything was the matter. "Nothing more than a change of *mind*, my dear"—and he was gone.

10.

Reclaiming the Spirit of the Founders

Conclusion

Toward the end of his life, James Madison wondered if he and his generation had become obsolete. "Having outlived so many of my contemporaries," he mused, "I ought not to forget that I may be thought to have outlived myself." Are the ideas of Madison and his compatriots passé?

Separated from the last of the founders by a span of almost two hundred years, today's readers might ask whether the spiritual precepts that guided these revolutionary spirits remain relevant to the twenty-first century, or whether like so many other artifacts of eighteenth-century life—from Jefferson's polygraph to Paine's smokeless candle—their convictions are of antiquarian interest only.

Two common misconceptions surround America's founders. One is that they were devout believers, intent upon establishing a godly nation. This misunderstanding persists because many of the original settlers of North America were indeed defiantly Christian. Especially among dissenting congregations that had broken with the Church of England, opposition to British authority was a long-standing habit. Treasuring their spiritual independence, they were inflamed by what they perceived as England's high-handed treatment of the colonies. Fears that the mother country might even try to establish an Anglican Episcopate in the New World fueled support for separation among Baptists, Congregationalists, Presbyterians, and other Reformed churches that sought liberty to follow their own interpretation of the Bible. These religious resisters formed an important part of the backbone of the American Revolution.

But the founding fathers were influenced less by biblical religion than by the intellectual awakening known as the Enlightenment, and this leads to the second misconception. Many mistakenly suppose that men like Benjamin Franklin, Thomas Jefferson, and Thomas Paine were of a wholly secular bent, or that their religious beliefs—if they had any—were lukewarm or lightly held. Deism is often typified as a cerebral and cold-blooded philosophy, without power to touch the inward springs. And it is true that the European Enlightenment took an irreligious turn. So the error is explicable. But the Enlightenment in America was seldom atheistic; more often it was soulful, earnest, and intensely moral. Though the men who founded America questioned doctrines they considered doubtful, they each developed a spiritual stance that enabled them to live with zest and face death with dignity and courage.

Their faith was flavored by science. Emboldened by the breakthroughs of Newton, they believed the unassisted intellect could plumb the mysteries of the universe, apart from any revelation. They were practical types—engineers, architects, farmers, physicians, surveyors, and military men. This meant they were results oriented, less interested in the maze of theological speculation than in the tangible difference faith made in the lives of its adherents. In addition, many were lawyers who felt that religion should appeal to the same kind of hardheaded arguments that would hold up in a courtroom. Rejecting supernaturalism, they sought down-to-earth explanations for how the world worked. They found God in nature—in the stately order of her laws, in the rituals of sowing and reaping that made agriculture so deeply satisfying, and in the natural endowments of the human mind, especially in the voice of conscience.

They believed the curtain was opening on a bright new day. A providential hand was guiding America toward a better future. None of our founders felt they were living near the end times or that God's judgment was about to bring history to a close. They were sure that an era of moral and political, as well as scientific, progress was in the offing. James Madison, for example, saw no reason why constitutional systems like the one he engineered might not eventually spread to create a federation of the world. "All eyes are opened, or opening to the rights of man," averred Thomas Jefferson. "The general spread of the light of science has already laid open to every view the palpable truth that the mass of mankind has not been born, with saddles on their backs." Anticipating the diffusion of democracy became a warm and stirring gospel. When the Constitutional Convention adjourned in Philadelphia in September 1787, Benjamin Franklin observed that the rear of the moderator's chair was decorated with a depiction of the sun resting on the horizon. Throughout the difficult deliberations, he had wondered whether it portrayed dusk or dawn. With the Constitution completed and ready for ratification, he was confident that the scene represented a rising, not a setting sun.

Feeling they were part of history's vanguard fired them with an almost selfless zeal. They did not profiteer from war or public office. Jefferson told one correspondent that he completed his years of national service with "hands as clean as they are empty." The plow he designed, with a moldboard mathematically sculpted to offer least resistance in turning the soil, vastly improved a device little changed since Roman times, but was never patented. Like his cohorts, the inventor was less motivated by hope of personal gain than by desire to benefit humanity.

The spirit of the Enlightenment lived on briefly after their demise. James Monroe, the Revolutionary War hero who followed Madison into the White House in 1817, was probably even more skeptical toward the claims of creedal Christianity than his predecessors—although even more off the record about his beliefs. John Quincy Adams, who had seen Redcoats drilling on the Boston Common and witnessed the Battle of Bunker Hill as a boy, was decidedly more conventional than his father, but indicated that he would knock down any minister who dared to preach hell and damnation from the pulpit. He was just as fascinated with astronomy as the elder Adams, and during his presidency (1825–29) lobbied for a system of national observatories or "lighthouses in the sky," a proposal that was roundly ridiculed. John Quincy was also the last to labor for a national university—a dream of enlightened chief executives ever since the Washington administration.

But the times were changing, as religious revivals swept across America in the first quarter of the nineteenth century. Only one in eight Americans claimed membership in a church in the period leading up to the Revolution, even in Puritan New England. But in the decades that followed, collaborations like the American Bible Society (1816) and American Tract Society (1825) were organized to carry the gospel to the unchurched. Evangelicals saw a surge in numbers, especially on the frontier, where itinerant preachers were welcomed as emissaries of civilization. In 1832, Alexis de Tocqueville remarked on the pervasive sway of piety he discovered during his tour of the United States. Harriet Martineau, who called on an aged James Madison when she visited the country three years later, also noticed that Americans were almost all proselytes to one denomination or another. "One circumstance struck me throughout the country. Almost as often as the conversation between myself and any other person on religious subjects became intimate and earnest, I was met by the supposition that I was a convert. This fact speaks volumes."

John Adams survived long enough to witness the missionary upsurge, deploring it as among the "distempers" to which humankind was liable. "We have now, it seems, a National Bible Society, to propagate the King James Bible, through all Nations," he complained to Thomas Jefferson in 1816. "Would it not be better, to apply these pious Subscriptions, to purify Christendom from the Corruptions of Christianity; than to propagate these Corruptions in Europe, Asia, Africa and

America?" From Monticello, the resident sage agreed completely that these "incendiaries" ought rather to amend their own religion than try to change that of others. Yet both men had helped to create conditions where, by the end of their lifetimes, proselytizing and missions might thrive. By defining the individual as a spiritual free agent within an unregulated religious marketplace, the founders opened the field to revivalists vying to save souls by whatever means possible—promises of heaven or threats of hell packaged in terms the roughest pioneer could comprehend.

A changing theology propelled America's conversion. An earlier generation held that only God could deliver sinners into a state of grace. There was little human beings could do to hasten or prevent a dynamic of redemption that was entirely in the hands of the Almighty. But evangelists in the nineteenth century agreed that a more popular, extemporaneous preaching style might help ready the reprobate to receive the divine influx. Droning sermons gave way to more dramatic altar calls. Showmanship entered the pulpit. The two former presidents with their high-minded, philosophic discourse were at a persuasive disadvantage.

Freethinking went out of fashion. Thomas Jefferson had predicted to Benjamin Waterhouse in 1822 that "there is not a young man now living in the United States who will not die a Unitarian." John Locke's rationalistic theology would prevail in religion, Jefferson presumed, just as Lockean principles of governance had displaced feudalism and the divine right of kings. But putting so much faith in reason was not entirely reasonable. For if the opening phases of the Enlightenment belonged to the optimistic Locke, the closing decades were shaped by his less sanguine successor David Hume (1711–76), who concluded that reason alone led to the impasse of absolute skepticism. In his *Dialogues Concerning Natural Religion*, Hume argued the impossibility of deriving any knowledge of God or his attributes from the study of nature: "A total suspense of judgment is here our only reasonable resource." All beliefs were equally arbitrary, and while the Scottish philosopher himself tended toward agnosticism ("Generally speaking, the errors in religion are dangerous; those in philosophy only ridiculous"), preferring one theological system to another was more a matter of custom and convenience than of strict logic.

But if the head was an unreliable guide, why not trust the heart? The starry firmament still dazzled the sight and sunlight warmed the flesh. About that there seemed no doubt. But rather than displacing more traditional worship, communing with the divine through Creation remained a mostly private epiphany, without any strong institutional ties. Natural religion exerted an ongoing literary influence through the writings of Ralph Waldo Emerson (1803–82), and other Transcendentalists, but its epistemology was romanticized from a faith grounded in observation and experiment to one based on feeling and intuition. Favoring the promptings of the spirit over the marshaling of evidence, the religion of Concord in this respect was not so different from the emotionalism of the camp meetings; the founders would have found both overwrought. The Age of Reason was in retreat.

Masonry became the target of strange conspiracy theories. In 1826, a certain William Morgan from Batavia, New York, claimed to have penetrated the sinister secrets of the brotherhood, but before he could publish his findings, he unaccountably disappeared. Foul play was suspected, and anti-Masonry became the platform for a third political party, entering the presidential sweepstakes in 1832 and winning about 8 percent of the popular vote. Churches declared a crusade, and preachers joined the bandwagon. The Reverend Lebbeus Armstrong of the Presbyterian Church in Northampton, New York, sermonized on "Masonry Proved to Be a Work of Darkness, Repugnant to the Christian Religion," while another minister in Ohio intoned upon "Solomon's Temple Haunted, or Free Masonry, the Man of Sin in the Temple of God." Masonry had originated as an attempt to bridge religious differences and quell internecine bickering by putting faith on a more empirical foundation. But that grand design was crumbling. The fellowship that John Desaguliers launched and that Washington felt held such promise for the future fell under a shadow.

The first president's own memory was being hijacked. At Washington's passing, orators compared him to a living god, "Columbia's second Savior," and the tributes only became more inflated. The fledgling country was in need of heroes and liked them spotless. Abigail Adams fumed at what she called "a mad rant of bombast," remarking that simple truth was Washington's best and greatest eulogy. But a process of deification was transforming the first president from flesh-and-blood mortal into a national icon.

At the same time, his beliefs were being distorted by biographers like Parson Weems, who reframed Washington's life and death as a Christian morality tale—the man who could not tell a lie, or think a heterodox thought. Following his *Life of Washington Together With Curious Anecdotes Equally Honorable to Himself & Exemplary to His Young Countrymen* in 1800, Weems sketched out *The Life of Benjamin Franklin* in 1817. The parson assured readers that while the philosopher was a bit offbeat in some of his notions, he was "very much a Christian in his practice." Franklin probably wouldn't have minded being called a practicing Christian; he had been called much worse. But without delving into any of old Ben's actual opinions, Weems went further: "Nor is it indeed to be wondered at that a man of doctor Franklin's extraordinary sagacity, born and brought up under the light of the Gospel, should have imbibed its spirit, and got his whole soul enriched, and as it were interlarded, with its benevolent affections." The founders were being spiritually sanitized, a process that still continues. Even now, some try to recast America's revolutionary forebears as born again.

In fact, they were religious liberals who respected the Bible, but criticized and revised scriptural teachings to meet the needs of the modern world. None of the figures featured in this book defined themselves or their country in exclusively Christian terms. Few could have foreseen the burgeoning bazaar of spiritual practice that marks the contemporary scene, where Buddhists rival Episcopalians and Muslims have overtaken Presbyterians in the nation's religious census. But the founders were no strangers to multiculturalism, either. As secretary of state in 1805, James Madison simultaneously entertained Sidi Suliman Mellimelli, the ambassador from Tunis, along with representatives of the Creek, Osage, Sac, Sioux, and Missouri tribes in his F Street parlor in Washington—the one berobed in flowing crimson with hookah-carrying attendants, the others baring skin, with painted faces and feathered topknots. The ambassador demanded to know who the Indians believed in—Abraham, Jesus, or Muhammad? Through an interpreter, the chieftains replied that they worshiped the Great Spirit without intermediaries, a response that provoked puzzled exasperation from the Tunisian but probably elicited only a sympathetic smile from their genial host. Though less diverse than today, the United States even at its inception included a medley of creeds and folkways. And the system the Constitution's framers devised to bring decency and order to the public square made no assumptions of religious uniformity.

The founders were ahead of their time, and far from being outmoded, their ideas still have a progressive ring. Over two centuries ago, James Madison wrote a treatise on "Population and Emigration," pointing out that the human species has the ability to procreate in numbers that might eventually outrun the earth's ability to feed and support them all. Presciently, he foresaw the United States approaching two hundred million inhabitants by the middle of the twentieth century, with similar increases elsewhere. Worried about the planet's long-term carrying capacity, he was an early advocate of what would now be called sustainable farming: contour plowing, crop rotation, and other techniques for stewarding the land. As president of the Agricultural Society of Albemarle, Virginia, he recognized that nature exists in a delicate balance that cannot be upset without dire consequences. Pure, clean air he acknowledged as vital to the support of biological systems, for example. Soil conservation and preservation of forests were necessary for the long-term health of human communities. As a proponent of scientific agriculture, Madison was optimistic about people's capacity to prosper and raise standards of living, but also knew that nature has limits that must be respected. Wise stewards work with the earth instead of against it. Reverence for the environment, or what might now be called eco-spirituality, was a part of natural religion.

Thomas Jefferson was equally farsighted in his notion of "posterity rights." The dead had no rightful power to burden the living with debts they could not pay or saddle them with intolerable legal arrangements. Children should not be required to pay for the extravagances and wasteful wars of their parents and predecessors. Jefferson proposed that every law (and even a nation's constitution) should be required to "sunset" with the passage of time, to free the present from the hand of the past. Like Madison, he was an ecological prophet. Anticipating concerns now coming to the fore, he inquired whether large-scale deforestation might eventually affect the climate. He suggested temperature and precipitation surveys be undertaken at hundred-year or fifty-year intervals to measure the impacts of clearing the land and human settlement. The earth belongs to the living, Jefferson held. But it is only held in trust. We have no right to despoil nature—and a positive obligation to pass on a viable future to those who come after us.

As he looked beyond his lifetime, George Washington was acutely conscious of how his actions as president would set precedents for the future and worried about the impact of his decisions on what he called the "unborn Millions." Consistent with his largesse, he gifted Liberty Hall in Lexington, Virginia, with the largest endowment ever given to a college at the time. Now known as Washington and Lee University, the school's motto remains *non incautus futuri*—"not unmindful of the future."

And in his will, Benjamin Franklin acknowledged the seventh generation in his own inimitable manner. He put a small part of his estate—the amount he would have earned as governor of Pennsylvania, had he accepted any salary for his service—in trust, to be distributed on the bicentennial of his death. Two centuries later, the sum had grown to over seven million dollars, disbursed freely to benefit a range of scholarship programs, museums, public libraries, and fire brigades. Franklin would have been pleased, but not surprised, for he had planned it that way. He knew the great purpose of a life is to spend it for something that outlasts it.

Imagining the impact of one's actions hundreds of years hence requires a spiritual leap—an act of faith. These were men who thought long-term, envisioning the repercussions of their deeds on those still unborn and descendants yet to come.

We are the beneficiaries of their foresight and generosity. To the extent citizens of the United States now enjoy the blessings of freedom and a measure of civility among those of divergent faiths, we can thank the revolutionary spirits who set the country on its present course, building a firm boundary of separation between church and state so that religion in the private sphere could attain its present vigor and variety. Though they did not seek to found a Christian nation, they did aim to establish a republic of virtue, and we must never forget their conviction that civic virtue implies not only tolerance but respect for the multiplicity of opinions and outlooks that infuse this land. Diversity, they taught, is the nation's strength. Taking that spiritual legacy for granted would be both ungracious and dangerous. The values and core beliefs of the founders need to be better known and more vigilantly defended if we wish the system of government they established—and the liberties they bequeathed us—to endure.

Endnotes

CHAPTER 1

P. 5-6 "The figures singled out here are representative: Benjamin Franklin (1706–90), George Washington (1732–99), Thomas Paine (1737–1809), John Adams (1735–1826), Thomas Jefferson (1743–1826), and James Madison (1751–1836)." The historian Charles Beard identified these six as primary among the founders, based on their spiritual affinity and preeminence in the American cause. "When the crisis came, Jefferson, Paine, John Adams, Washington, Franklin, Madison and many lesser lights were to be reckoned among either the Unitarians or the Deists. It was not Cotton Mather's God to whom the authors of the Declaration of Independence appealed; it was to 'Nature's God.'" Charles A. Beard and Mary R. Beard, *The Rise of American Civilization, Volume I*, Macmillan Co., New York, p. 449.

CHAPTER 2

P. 14 For Alexis de Tocqueville's observations on separation of church and state, see *Democracy in America*, J. P. Mayer (ed.), Anchor Books, Garden City, NY, p. 295.

P. 14 "The framers believed that an official hands-off policy toward religion would unleash people's latent spiritual energies, just as a laissez-faire policy toward the economy would unlock the engine of private enterprise." Frank Lambert, in *The Founding Fathers and the Place of Religion in America*, Princeton University Press, Princeton, NJ, 2003, p. 138, points out that Christian evangelicals during the eighteenth century also used marketplace metaphors to describe their trade, adopting advertising and newspaper promotion to heighten their proselytizing's effectiveness. "A consumer revolution in the English Atlantic provided evangelicals with new models for defining their audiences and new techniques of conveying the gospel to them."

P. 16 "During its state convention to ratify the federal constitution, a Virginia initiative tried to change the wording and intent of this clause to "no *other* religious test shall ever be required *than* a belief in the one only true God, who is the rewarder of the good, and the punisher of evil." There were many attempts to insert theological language into the U.S.

Constitution during the ratification process and in the years following. See Isaac Kramnick and R. Laurence Moore, *The Godless Constitution: The Case Against Religious Correctness*, W.W. Norton & Company, New York, 1996, p. 146 ff.

P. 17 "All believed in God, after their own fashion. But their intent was never to establish a godly commonwealth or Christian nation." The secular basis for the United States government was clear in the minds of the founders and found explicit expression in the Treaty of Tripoli, negotiated in 1796 between America and the Barbary states, approved by John Adams and ratified by the U.S. Senate the following year. Article Two of the treaty states that "the government of the United States of America is not in any sense founded on the Christian Religion."

P. 22 "One of the finest scenes and subjects of religious contemplation is to walk into the woods and fields. . . ." Paine's words are from an essay titled "Of the Sabbath-Day in Connecticut," included in Norman Cousins, *In God We Trust: The Religious Beliefs and Ideas of the American Founding Fathers*, Harper & Brothers Publishers, New York, 1958, p. 432.

P. 24 For Jefferson's "pillow of ignorance," see Henry May, *The Enlightenment in America*, Oxford University Press, New York, 1986, p. 297.

CHAPTER 3

P. 32 Information on the history of ordeal by touch can be found in "Ordeal by Touch" by Lawrence B. Custer in *American Heritage Magazine*, April/May 1986, Volume 37, Issue 3. Details concerning the trial in Boxford, Massachusetts, can be found in *Everyday Life in the Massachusetts Bay Colony* by George Dow, Dover Publications, 1988.

P. 34 "Astrology has a Philosophical Foundation. . . ." The citation is from Keith Cerniglia, "The American Almanac and the Astrology Factor," http://earlyamerica.com/review/2003_winter_spring/almanac.htm, p. 6. Another resource on this topic can be found in "Information of the Unlearned: The Enlightenment in Early American Almanacs, 1650–1800," by Daniel Winik in *The Concord Review*, www.tcr.org/tcr/essays.htm.

P. 37 "Ignorant Men wonder how we Astrologers foretell the Weather so exactly. . . ." See *Poor Richard's Almanack, 1739*. Franklin's words are quoted in Daniel Winik, "Information of the Unlearned: The Enlightenment in Early American Almanacs, 1650-1800," in *The Concord Review*, www.tcr.org/tcr/essays.htm.

Endnotes

P. 38 Dolley Madison's penchant for horoscopes is discussed in Virginia Moore, *The Madisons: A Biography*, McGraw-Hill Book Company, New York, 1979, p. 210.

P. 40 "The clanking of chains, and the noise of the whip, are no longer heard in their cells. . . ." See Carl Binger, *Revolutionary Doctor: Benjamin Rush, 1746–1813*, W.W. Norton & Co., New York, 1966, p. 279.

CHAPTER 4

P. 52 The text of Franklin's revision of the Lord's Prayer can be found in Norman Cousins, *op. cit.*, p. 21.

P. 54 ". . . Priestley emigrated to Franklin's home city of Philadelphia." On July 14, 1791, Joseph Priestley had gathered with friends of Tom Paine and other supporters of the French Revolution to celebrate the anniversary of the storming of the Bastille, when his home and laboratory were attacked by mobs. For details, see John Keane's *Tom Paine: A Political Life*, Grove Press, New York, 1995, p. 320.

P. 55 The effects of Whitefield's preaching are described in Benjamin Franklin, *Autobiography of Benjamin Franklin*, Yale University Press, New Haven, CT, 1964, p. 177.

P. 56 "I have lived, Sir, a long time, and the longer I live, the more convincing proofs I see of this truth—that God governs in the affairs of men." See Benjamin Franklin, *Writings*, Library of America, New York, pp. 1138–1139.

P. 57 "I think the system of morals and his religion, as he left them to us, the best the world ever saw or is likely to see. . . ." This letter to Ezra Stiles can be found in Cousins, *op. cit.*, p. 42.

P. 57 For the full text of the "Articles of Belief and Acts of Religion," see Benjamin Franklin, *The Papers of Benjamin Franklin, Volume I*, Leonard Labaree (ed.), Yale University Press, New Haven, CT, 1959, pp. 101–109.

P. 58 "For Peace and Liberty, for Food and Raiment, for Corn and Wine, And Milk, and every kind of Healthful Nourishment, *Good God I Thank thee*." For Franklin's prayer, see *ibid.*

CHAPTER 5

P. 66 For Washington's effect on Abigail Adams, see Page Smith, *John Adams, Volume I, 1735–1784*, Doubleday & Company, Garden City, NY, 1962, p. 201.

P. 69 "And while his 'Providence' sounded like the kind of higher power that might answer prayers, he also spoke of the governing power behind events as a stern necessity, impervious to supplication." Washington referred to providence with a variety of pronouns: *he*, *she*, or even *it*.

P. 69-70 For a full accounting of George Washington's views on the afterlife, see the article by Peter Henriques, "The Final Struggle between George Washington and the Grim King: Washington's Attitude toward Death and an Afterlife" in Don Higginbotham, *George Washington Reconsidered*, University of Virginia Press, Charlottesville, VA, 2001.

P. 74 The Masonic Constitution can be found in Bernard Fay, *Revolution and Freemasonry 1680–1800*, Little, Brown & Company, Boston, 1935, p. 110.

P. 75 "Giving and receiving letters of business, reading Advertisements. . . ." This description of Sunday morning activity is documented in Lambert, *op. cit.*, p. 59.

P. 76 "One Sunday in November 1789, shortly after he had been elected president. . . ." Rev. E. C. M'Guire, married to the daughter of Washington's nephew and private secretary, and therefore in a position to know, states that Washington on this occasion came near to "being arrested." M'Guire, *The Religious Opinions and Character of Washington*, 1836, p. 175, cited in *George Washington the Christian* by William J. Johnson, Abingdon Press, New York, 1919, p. 176.

P. 77 For Rector Abercrombie's letter, note Rupert Hughes, *George Washington: Savior of the States 1777–1781*, William Morrow and Company, New York, 1930, p. 285.

P. 78 "He seldom mentioned Jesus." George Washington deliberately avoided using the name of Christ in his prayers. In 1776, for example, Congress called for a day of prayer among the troops "to confess and bewail our manifold sins and transgressions . . . and, through the merits and mediation of Jesus Christ, obtain his pardon and forgiveness." Washington deliberately altered the language to omit the last phrase. Instead, he invited the soldiers to "supplicate the mercy of Almighty God, that it would please him to pardon all our manifold sins and transgressions, and to prosper the arms of the United Colonies." The following year, Congress asked that another day be set aside to pray for forgiveness "through the merits of Jesus Christ." Washington's orders substituted a "publick Thanksgiving and praise & Duty calling us Devoutly to Express our grateful acknowledgments to God for the manifold blessing he has granted us." See Rupert Hughes, *ibid.*, p. 292.

Endnotes

P. 79 "The Rev. John Murray is appointed Chaplain to the Rhode Island Regiments, and is to be respected as such." See George Washington, *The Writings of George Washington, Volume 3, January 1770–September 1775*, John Fitzpatrick (ed.), U.S. Government Printing Office, p. 497. George and Martha were subscribers to the *Gleaner*, written by John Murray's wife Judith Sargent Murray—perhaps an indication of where their own sympathies lay. See Russell Miller, *The Larger Hope: The First Century of the Universalist Church in America, 1770–1870*, Unitarian Universalist Association, Boston, 1979, p. 29.

P. 80 ". . . the vestry was more a civil office than an ecclesiastical one at that time. . . ." Doing duty as a vestryman was a social expectation for well-born Virginians and did not necessarily reflect any specific religious commitment. Thomas Jefferson, who was far from being an orthodox Christian, served on his local vestry, just like Washington. And when George Washington announced his intention to retire from public life at the conclusion of the Revolutionary War, he resigned from every post that might be considered a civil office, including the vestry.

P. 84 The Farewell Address has its own fascinating history. Portions of George Washington's Farewell were written by James Madison and Alexander Hamilton. The passages pertaining to religion probably originated with Hamilton, and Washington softened and tempered some of his more dogmatic language. For example, Hamilton's draft asserted that we ought not "to flatter ourselves that morality can be separated from religion." Washington effectively reversed this statement, changing the wording to "Let us with caution indulge the supposition that morality can be maintained without religion." See Forrest Church, *The Separation of Church and State: Writings on a Fundamental Freedom by America's Founders*, Beacon Press, Boston, 2004, p. 113.

Chapter 6

P. 94 "Near three thousand years passed away from the Mosaic account of the creation till the Jews under a national delusion requested a king. . . ." Thomas Paine, *Political Writings*, Bruce Kuklick (ed.), Cambridge University Press, Cambridge, England, 1989, p. 9.

P. 95 "The summer soldier and the sunshine patriot. . . ." Jack Fruchtman Jr., *Thomas Paine: Apostle of Freedom*, Four Walls Eight Windows, New York, 1994, p. 90.

P. 102 "Does not the creation, the universe we behold, preach to us the existence of an Almighty power, that governs and regulates the whole?" The passage is from Thomas Paine, *Age of Reason,* cited in Cousins, *op. cit.*, p. 401.

P. 104 "I believe in one God and no more. . . ." *Ibid.*, p. 395.

P. 108 "The world is my country, All mankind are my brethren. . . ." *Ibid.*, p. 394.

CHAPTER 7

P. 114 "There is a dreadful fiery hell. . . ." Page Smith, *John Adams, Volume I, 1735–1784*, Doubleday & Company, Garden City, NY, 1962, p. 11.

P. 118 "We can never be so certain of any prophecy. . . ." Norman Cousins, *op. cit.*, p. 239. The citation is in a letter from Adams to Thomas Jefferson, written September 14, 1813.

P. 120 "Our system, considered as one body hanging on its center of gravity. . . ." Cousins, *ibid.*, p. 84. The passage is from an entry in Adams's diary, dated May 1, 1756.

P. 121 "My adoration of the Author of the Universe is too profound and too sincere. . . ." Cousins, *ibid.*, p. 240. The quotation is from the letter of September 14, 1813, cited above.

P. 126 "My religion is founded on the love of God and my neighbor. . . ." Cousins, *ibid.*, p. 103. The excerpt is from Adams's letter to F.A. Van der Kamp, dated July 13, 1815.

P. 127 The epitaph to Henry Adams can be found in David McCollough, *John Adams*, Simon & Schuster, New York, 2001, p. 649.

CHAPTER 8

P. 132 "Let the standard of measure, then, be a uniform, cylindrical rod of iron. . . ." Dumas Malone, *Jefferson and the Rights of Man*, Little, Brown and Company, Boston, 1951, p. 277.

P. 134 "A Decalogue of Canons" Silvio Bedini, *Thomas Jefferson: Statesman of Science*, Macmillan Publishing Company, New York, 1990, p. 13.

P. 135 "How sublime to look down into the workhouse of nature. . . ." Noble Cunningham Jr., *In Pursuit of Reason: The Life of Thomas Jefferson*, Ballantine Books, New York, 1987, p. 20.

Endnotes

P. 141 "In politics he would recognize the universal brotherhood of man under the fatherhood of God; at the same time he would love his country and hold himself ready to die at any time to avert its disgrace or his own." Will Durant, *Caesar and Christ: A History of Roman Civilization and of Christianity from Their Beginnings to A.D. 325 (The Story of Civilization III)*, Simon and Schuster, New York, 1944, p. 300.

P. 143 "In this state of things among the Jews, Jesus appeared. . . ." Dumas Malone, *Jefferson the President, First Term*, Little, Brown and Company, Boston, 1970, p. 202.

P. 147 A "Death Bed Adieu" Bedini, *op. cit.*, p. 479.

P. 152 "I am happy to be able to inform you that we have now in the United States a negro . . ." Bedini, *op. cit.*, p. 222.

P. 154 "Indeed I tremble for my country when I reflect that God is just. . . ." For this quotation and Jefferson's further thoughts on slavery, see the *Notes on the State of Virginia* in Thomas Jefferson's *Writings*, Martin Segal (ed.), Library of America, New York, 1984, p. 289.

CHAPTER 9

P. 160 For the syllogisms from the "Book of Logick," see Irving Brant, *James Madison: The Virginia Revolutionist*, Bobbs-Merrill Company, New York, 1951, p. 62.

P. 160 "At Robertson's school, young Madison penned a diagram titled 'The Solar System from Copernicus,' showing planets ranging from Mercury to Saturn, surrounded by their respective satellites and accompanied by each object's distance from the sun." Many historians think these astronomical diagrams were done later, when Madison was at Princeton. Irving Brant dates them to the time Madison spent at Robertson's academy. See Brant, *ibid.*, p. 60.

P. 166 "That religion, or the duty which we owe our Creator, and the manner of discharging it, can be directed only by reason and conviction. . . ." Ralph Ketcham, *James Madison: A Biography*, University of Virginia Press, Charlottesville, VA, p. 73.

P. 167 "Because experience witnesseth that ecclesiastical establishments, instead of maintaining the purity and efficacy of Religion. . . ." Cousins, *op. cit.*, p. 311. The citation is from Madison's Memorial and Remonstrance.

P. 168 "If men were angels, no government would be necessary. . . ." Federalist Number 51 in Alexander Hamilton, John Jay, James Madison, *The Federalist*, Modern Library, New York, p. 337.

P. 170 ". . . neither had been to church in many years." See Ketcham, *op. cit.*, p. 324.

P. 175 ". . . Madison was inducted into the American Philosophical Society along with Joseph Priestley and Tom Paine." Thomas Jefferson, John Adams, and George Washington had all been previously inducted on January 21, 1780.

P. 175 "I was never at Mr. Madison's but once. . . ." This quotation from Bishop Meade can be found in Brant, *op. cit.*, p. 113.

P. 176 "I concur with you at once in rejecting the idea maintained by some divines. . . ." See Irving Brant, *James Madison: Commander in Chief*, Bobbs-Merrill Company, New York, 1961, p. 445.

P. 179 "As president, Madison remained determined to keep government at arm's length from organized religion." In 1811, James Madison vetoed a bill to incorporate a church within the District of Columbia on grounds that the measure violated the First Amendment; for the same reason, he blocked a congressional grant of public land to a small Baptist church in Mississippi. By the end of his life, he came to believe that appointing chaplains to Congress and the armed forces also crossed the line that should separate church and state.

CHAPTER 10

P. 193 "The founders were being spiritually sanitized. . . ." The Harvard historian Perry Miller observes that in 1800, "amid the great revivals which swept over Connecticut, Kentucky, and Tennessee in that year, which expanded into Georgia, Illinois, and for decades burned over northern New York, the Revolution was again and again presented as having been itself a majestic revival. The leadership of Jefferson, Paine and the rationalists was either ignored or explained away." See Perry Miller, *Nature's Nation*, Harvard University Press, Cambridge, MA, 1967, p. 108.

Bibliography

Barker, Charles A., *American Convictions: Cycles of Public Thought 1600–1800*, J. S. Lippincott Company, Philadelphia and New York, 1970.

Beard, Charles A., and Mary R. Beard, *The Rise of American Civilization: Volume I, The Agricultural Era*, The Macmillan Company, New York, 1927.

Bedini, Silvio, *Thomas Jefferson: Statesman of Science*, Macmillan Publishing Company, New York, 1990.

Bennett, Lerone, Jr., *Before the Mayflower: A History of Black America*, Penguin Books, New York, 1982.

Binger, Carl, *Revolutionary Doctor: Benjamin Rush, 1746–1813*, W.W. Norton & Co., New York, 1966.

Boorstin, Daniel J., *The Discoverers: A History of Man's Search to Know His World and Himself*, Random House, New York, 1983.

Brady, Patricia, *Martha Washington: An American Life*, Penguin Group, New York, 2005.

Brands, H. W., *The First American: The Life and Times of Benjamin Franklin*, Doubleday, New York, 2000.

Brant, Irving, *James Madison: The Virginia Revolutionist*, Bobbs-Merrill Company, New York, 1941.

_____, *James Madison: The Nationalist*, Bobbs-Merrill Company, New York, 1948.

_____, *James Madison: Father of the Constitution*, Bobbs-Merrill Company, New York, 1950.

_____, *James Madison: Commander in Chief*, Bobbs-Merrill Company, New York, 1961.

Bratton, Fred Gladstone, *The Legacy of the Liberal Spirit*, Beacon Press, Boston, 1960.

Brauer, Jerald, *Religion and the American Revolution*, Fortress Press, Philadelphia, 1976.

Bibliography

Brookhiser, Richard, *What Would the Founders Do?* Perseus Books, New York, 2006.

Church, Forrest, *The Separation of Church and State: Writings on a Fundamental Freedom by America's Founders*, Beacon Press, Boston, 2004.

Cohen, Bernard, *Science and the Founding Fathers*, W.W. Norton & Co., New York, 1995.

Commager, Henry Steele, *The Empire of Reason: How Europe Imagined and America Realized the Enlightenment*, Anchor Press, Garden City, NY, 1977.

Cone, Carl, *Torchbearer of Freedom: The Influence of Richard Price on Eighteenth-Century Thought*, University of Kentucky Press, Lexington, KY, 1952.

Cousins, Norman (ed.), *In God We Trust: The Religious Beliefs and Ideas of the American Founding Fathers*, Harper & Brothers, New York, 1958.

Cunningham, Noble Jr., *In Pursuit of Reason: The Life of Thomas Jefferson*, Ballantine Books, New York, 1987.

Dinnerstein, Leonard and Kenneth Jackson (eds.), *American Vistas 1607–1877*, Oxford University Press, Oxford, England, 1983.

Dray, Philip, *Stealing God's Thunder: Benjamin Franklin's Lightening Rod and the Invention of America*, Random House, New York, 2005.

Durant, Will, *Caesar and Christ: A History of Roman Civilization and of Christianity from Their Beginnings to A.D. 325*, Simon and Schuster, New York, 1944.

_____, *The Age of Louis XIV: A History of European Civilization in the Period of Pascal, Molière, Cromwell, Milton, Peter the Great, Newton and Spinoza: 1648–1715*, Simon and Schuster, New York, 1963.

Ellis, Joseph, *His Excellency: George Washington*, Alfred Knopf, New York, 2004.

Engeman, Thomas, and Michael Zuckert (eds.), *Protestantism and the American Founding*, University of Notre Dame Press, Notre Dame, IN, 2004.

Fay, Bernard, *Revolution and Freemasonry 1680–1800,* Little, Brown & Company, Boston, 1935.

Flexner, James Thomas, *Washington: The Indispensable Man*, Little, Brown & Company, Boston, 1969.

Bibliography

Franklin, Benjamin, *Autobiography of Benjamin Franklin*, Yale University Press, New Haven, CT, 1964.

_____, *The Papers of Benjamin Franklin*, Leonard Labaree (ed.), Yale University Press, New Haven, CT, 1959.

_____, *Writings*, Library of America, New York, 1987.

Fruchtman, Jack, Jr., *Thomas Paine: Apostle of Freedom*, Four Walls, Eight Windows, New York, 1994.

Gay, Peter, *The Enlightenment: An Interpretation, Volume II, The Science of Freedom*, Alfred Knopf, New York, 1969.

Gaustad, Edwin, *A Documentary History of Religion in America*, William Eerdmans Publishing Company, Grand Rapids, MI, 1982.

Gerson, Noel, *The Velvet Glove: A Life of Dolley Madison*, Thomas Nelson Publishers, New York, 1975.

Hamilton, Alexander, John Jay, and James Madison, *The Federalist*, Modern Library, New York.

Higginbotham, Don (ed.), *George Washington Reconsidered*, University of Virginia Press, Charlottesville, VA, 2001.

Holmes, David, *The Faiths of the Founding Fathers*, Oxford University Press, Oxford, England, 2006.

Hudson, Winthrop, *Religion in America*, Charles Scribner's Sons, New York, 1965.

Hughes, Rupert, *George Washington: The Human Being & The Hero*, William Morrow and Company, New York, 1926.

_____, *George Washington: The Rebel & The Patriot*, William Morrow and Company, New York, 1927.

_____, *George Washington: The Savior of the States 1777–1781*, William Morrow and Company, New York, 1930.

Isaacson, Walter, *Benjamin Franklin: An American Life*, Simon & Schuster, New York, 2003.

Jacob, Margaret, *The Radical Enlightenment: Pantheists, Freemasons and Republicans*, George Allen & Unwin, London, 1981.

Jefferson, Thomas, *Writings*, Martin Segal (ed.), Library of America, New York, 1984.

Keane, John, *Tom Paine: A Political Life*, Grove Press, New York, 1995.

Ketcham, Ralph, *James Madison: A Biography*, University Press of Virginia, Charlottesville, VA, 1990.

Koch, Adrienne, *Jefferson and Madison: The Great Collaboration*, Konecky & Konecky, Old Saybrook, CT.

Koch, G. Adolf, *Religion of the American Enlightenment*, Thomas Y. Crowell Company, New York, 1968.

Kramnick, Isaac, and R. Laurence Moore, *The Godless Constitution: The Case Against Religious Correctness*, W.W. Norton & Company, New York, 1996.

Lambert, Frank, *The Founding Fathers and the Place of Religion in America*, Princeton University Press, Princeton, NJ, 2003.

Locke, John, *An Essay Concerning Human Understanding*, in *The Empiricists*, Anchor Books, Garden City, NY 1974.

Malone, Dumas, *Jefferson the Virginian*, Little, Brown and Company, Boston, 1948.

_____, *Jefferson and the Rights of Man*, Little, Brown and Company, Boston, 1951.

_____, *Jefferson and the Ordeal of Liberty*, Little, Brown and Company, Boston, 1962.

_____, *Jefferson the President: First Term 1801–1805*, Little, Brown and Company, Boston, 1970.

_____, *Jefferson the President: Second Term 1805–1809*, Little, Brown and Company, Boston, 1974.

_____, *Jefferson and His Time: The Sage of Monticello*, Little, Brown and Company, 1981.

Mapp, Alf, Jr., *The Faiths of Our Fathers: What America's Founders Really Believed*, Rowman & Littlefield Publishers, Oxford, England, 2003.

May, Henry F., *The Enlightenment in America*, Oxford University Press, New York, 1986.

McCullough, David, *John Adams,* Simon & Schuster, New York, 2001.

McLoughlin, William, *New England Dissent 1630–1883*, Harvard University Press, Cambridge, MA, 1971.

Bibliography

Meacham, Jon, *American Gospel: God, the Founding Fathers, and the Making of a Nation*, Random House, New York, 2006.

Miller, Perry, *Nature's Nation*, Harvard University Press, Cambridge, MA, 1967.

Miller, Perry, and Thomas Johnson (eds.), *The Puritans: A Sourcebook of Their Writings, Volumes I and II*, Harper & Row, New York, 1963.

Miller, Russell, *The Larger Hope: The First Century of the Universalist Church in America, 1770–1870*, Unitarian Universalist Association, Boston, 1979.

Moore, Virginia, *The Madisons: A Biography*, McGraw-Hill Book Company, New York, 1979.

Novak, Michael, and Jana Novak, *Washington's God*, Basic Books, New York, 2006.

Paine, Thomas, *Common Sense and Other Political Writings*, Bobbs-Merrill Educational Publishing, Indianapolis, 1953.

_____, *The Rights of Man*, E.P. Dutton & Company, New York, 1915.

Peach, Bernard, *Richard Price and the Ethical Foundations of the American Revolution*, Duke University Press, Durham, NC, 1979.

Rakove, Jack, *James Madison and the Creation of the American Republic*, Scott, Foresman/Little, Brown Higher Education, Glenview, IL, 1990.

Randall, Willard Sterne, *George Washington: A Life*, Henry Holt & Company, New York, 1997.

Rutland, Robert, *James Madison, The Founding Father*, Macmillan Publishing Company, New York, 1987.

Sanford, Charles, *The Religious Life of Thomas Jefferson*, University of Virginia Press, Charlottesville, VA, 1984.

Smith, Page, *John Adams, Volume I, 1735–1784*, Doubleday & Company, Garden City, NY, 1962.

_____, *John Adams, Volume II, 1784–1826*, Doubleday & Company, Garden City, NY, 1962.

Tocqueville, Alexis de, *Democracy in America*, Anchor Books, Garden City, NY, 1969.

Washington, George, *Writings*, The Library of America, New York, 1997.

Bibliography

_____, *The Writings of George Washington, Volume Three, January 1770–September 1775,* John Fitzpatrick (ed.), U.S. Government Printing Office, 1931.

Wiencek, Henry, *An Imperfect God: George Washington, His Slaves, and the Creation of America*, Farrar, Straus and Giroux, New York, 2003.

Wills, Garry, *Cincinnatus: George Washington and the Enlightenment*, Doubleday & Company, Garden City, NY, 1984.

_____, *James Madison,* Henry Holt and Company, New York, 2002.

Wolf, Stephanie Grauman, *As Various As Their Land: The Everyday Lives of Eighteenth-Century Americans*, HarperCollins, New York, 1993.

Wood, Gordon, *Revolutionary Characters*, Penguin Press, New York, 2006.

Index

Index

Index